Strangely Wonderful.

By James Barrett Rodehaver

Strangely Wonderful.

Penhall Publishing

ISBN 978-0-9897893-0-1

Poetry/General

Poetry/Gay & Lesbian

Front cover painting by Christian Millet, photographed by Desmene Statum

Back cover photograph by Rosie Lindsey

Edited and designed for publication by Lilly Penhall, InterStellar Graphics

Dedication.

For Gary, Randy, Eric, Amber,
Corey, Mk and Desmene,

and for all those who
supported my dream.

This is for all the dreamers.
I knew I wasn't the only one.

Thank you all!

"You may say I'm a dreamer,
but I'm not the only one."

--- John Lennon, "Imagine."

Praise For
James Barrett Rodehaver:

"Unquestionably and unconditionally, Rodehaver's poetry is a testament of the raw power of the human will to survive and to bear witness to what it has survived. It is language in its most primal, bardic, shamanistic, and prophetic state; it is a *work of heart* that, in essence, both survives the radioactive event of itself and continues-- in its emotional honesty, sharp wit, and resonant dedication to self and others-- to be radioactive at its core."

M.K. Foster, Winner of the 2012 Gulf Coast Prize in Poetry

"James writes with passion and power; living his life out loud in these verses. His poetic perceptions will resonate with any and all who seek to make sense of what life brings along; reviling the senseless while revering the sensible. Read and identify!"

mh clay, Poetry Editor for Mad Swirl
www.madswirl.com

"James "Bear" Barrett Rodehaver's poetry will crack open the closed mind. The words of wisdom coming from this soul have touched my heart to the point of tears. The beautiful imagery and metaphoric mastery that Bear possesses will move even the most stagnant spirit. Bear is a STRONG activist for the LGBTQI community, and I feel honored to have been able to read his words, and hear him speak them."

Heidi 'Raw' Phillips-West, poet and novelist

"Bear says everything there is to say, from politics to philosophy to relationships to his own personal struggles. He weaves satiric stories that are both funny and thought-provoking, then tells a story of his own life that will break your heart but leave you full of hope. Witty, insightful, a little dirty and always making you think, his poetry will amaze you."

Lilly Penhall, poet, author of "O" and co-editor of Let It Bleed Zine

"A truly determined poet never existed, if ever before, James Barrett Rodehaver. His works are proof strength exists and that miracles happen. He possesses an aptitude for lyrics and verse rivaling Oscar Wilde. I'm so proud to know this brilliant young man, honored to have him as a part of my family, and am so grateful to be of any influence to him as a writer or a person."

Desmene Statum, poet, author of "Two-Fisted Whiskey Love Songs" and "Coagulation"

Strangely Wonderful.

Table of Contents

Inverted Reflection.

Looking down

into the still dark water,

ripples cut me into sections.

I find

that when I look into the cold waters of
my mind,

I see an inverted reflection.

I'm different than what you see.

I'm totally opposite of what you might
think.

I'm infested with thoughts and ideas,

crawling around inside my brain.

They are simple sparks of inspiration,

new arrows pointing new directions.

A disease of thought, of idea and of
mind.

A rapidly spreading mind infection.

Looking down, I see myself, an inverted
reflection.

Swarming and buzzing inside my head,

ideas and thoughts, how to change the
world.

Or how to change my own world instead.

I'm an oyster who's hiding this
beautiful pearl

of thought transformed from a tiny idea,
a tiny piece of sand.

That wedged its way inside my head, at
first, just

inspiration, but now something grand.

Dropping my idea into this pool,

inserting it there, I make the
connection,

the water it swirls and at last, it is
still.

Seeing myself an inverted reflection.

As a result of original thought,

the view that I see, it changes.

I see the world in a brand new way, my
life it now rearranges.

In the waters of life, of love and of
mind,

I see my reflection is inverted.

It's different from normal view of all
others, I find,

because of one new idea from which all
of this started.

So you see I am more different than
you'll ever know,

They try to figure me out, I perplex
them.

I'm opposite anything you've ever known,

look in my minds ocean and you will be
shown,

my world, which is swarming, and yet so
alone,

you can see my inverted reflection.

Self And Foe.

I battle the foe in myself,

not just good versus evil,

but brilliance versus stupidity;

the right words versus the wrong
thoughts;

Idea versus idea.

We fight on the green battlefield
inside,

blood-soaked from times that nobler
ideas have died,

and inner enemies slain in pride.

I fight my darker side with light,

it kicks and punches back, I cry,

and good intentions are outnumbered by

the reasons why I can do it later,

or other ideas with the illusion of
better.

And even if the good intentions do

finally get through; oh well,

they pave the way to hell,

which gives reason to say that
sometimes, some days,

procrastination and ideas that fail

are better than intentions that don't prevail,

and may be heaven-sent, imagine that!

I can do it later and call it moral;

but back on the field, my moral sword dulls,

it tries to hack away at sin,

but the blade is thin and dull, so then,

how can my sword be sharp again?

I should have been prepared before the war

with myself, but procrastination soars,

and I ask, "What am I fighting for?"

Still, other questions plague my fight.

Am I really on the side of right every time?

And if I battle me, am I hurting myself?

It sure feels like it.

The hero and the villain, in one,

Whoever wins, gets the body again,

and the weaker side of my self dies.

How many different pieces of me do lie

under this bloody field? No stone, for they

are only broken thoughts, dead ideas, morals that lost,

and ghosts of intention. And no matter how different

they all were, the blood's all mine, the pain's all too real,

I find myself slave to what I feel.

And still, I battle daily, as new ideas, babies,

grow and defend the things they represent,

and when battle does call them, they fight their brothers,

Oh, how grim!

And the final cost of peace,

my very death; the wars will cease.

For no new ideas or morals learned,

no more heroic mental medals earned,

for I am dust, as are they,

and under another battlefield, I'll lay.

Blood-stained in the spiritual way,

the ghosts of all I stood for, play

and haunt other minds from what they've
learned about my life,

and so people burn, as deep inside, a
battle ensues,

a vicious cycle of idealistic views
fighting,

and pitting self versus self,

a fight between their two inner sides,
and nobody else.

I battle the foe within myself: me.

And to create peace, I must cease to
exist,

my mind come to rest, my body be laid
low,

finally defeating both self, and foe!

The Suit.

I finish putting on my suit, and proceed
to walk out the door.

The hair unkempt, the teeth fanged
slightly,

the fingernails short and thin, half-
chewed.

The feet large and stumbling,

reminding me of Frankenstein with the
scars.

One hand swings uselessly, the other
poised with purpose,

ready to do all the work.

My knees weak and ready to bend to the
will

of gravity or any such force.

I stand listening for the change in the
wind,

promised eons ago by some blind prophet;

a living paradox standing between

the timeline and the hourglass.

My frame is small, my eyes the color of
oceans seeking depth.

The skin is light, mostly tender with
calloused parts,

and a good many scars.

A fading red line sliding down my chest,

reminder of the separation of two
halves,

the worst pain, which exposed the heart.

He is ready to speak, his tongue ready
to enunciate,

articulate, clarify and shout verses.

The suit fits tight over weary bones,

breaking with the strain of hard years.

I walk to the readings,

stand in my suit in front of my friends,
and read.

"Hello there, and welcome back," they
say.

This is my favorite suit, its strength
is in its weakness.

Not loving just the skin or the face, or
even the tongue,

but also how they are presented.

The clothes are trivial, all that
matters is the suit.

Someday, I will stand naked before you all,

baring only bones and poetry, for that is my soul.

Someday, I will cast this difficult and painful skin aside,

and stop lying.

Someday, I shall lose it all, only to gain myself.

When you see me then, do not cry or turn away;

this is me unadulterated, cold, honest

as a Sunday morning, free of crippling flesh.

When you see me, you will fall out of love with me,

for you only knew my trappings and facades.

You are in love with my suit,

and it is only protection from people in the world;

it is the mask which hides the truest scar.

I will cast the suit aside one day, and be alone, but free.

But for now, there is an event to attend,

a stage to stand on, people to impress,

a man I should continue to be.

So here I stand in the morning sun,

checking my suit for seamlessness, making sure

that my character flaws shine through just enough,

that my imperfections stay believable,

that my limp is true and painful with each step.

I stand here putting on this suit of mine,

this ball and chain which pulls me down, keeps

me humble, admirable, heroic in my fight.

I snap the last gnarled buttons of scarred flesh into place,

run out into the morning,

and stand in front of your crowds,

ironically to speak about being true to yourselves.

Every night when I go to bed, I pray
I'll wake up naked,

although it will alienate me
indefinitely.

The suit will have fully dissolved away
in lies,

like a hand in acid, leaving only the
bone,

and the memory of a hand.

Until then, it remains for reasons even
I do not fully

understand, and I wear it with a coy
sense of bitter pride;

limping my way into your hearts,

and writing a book of skin, to
complement this grim,

unassuming, and terrible suit.

Every button that nightly loosens brings
me closer to my soul,

and ever nearer to the bone.

Finding James.

Yes, I admit it,

I have been lost or hidden for years.

Stumbling in darkness, hiding from accusation and truth.

Lying to myself, lying to you, lying to all of you.

Living as both a miracle and as the great disappointer.

Is that an oxymoron?

No matter, all I know is, I'm lost, confused,

constantly searching for a sliver of hope that would tell me,

it's ok to be scared and lost, but keep keeping on.

I'd collect them in notebooks

as if they were stones or marbles;

trying to piece them together like a jigsaw puzzle of light

in a world of darkness and loss.

Maybe they'll form an answer, a way out,

a way to find the real James amongst all of the fake personas

I put on to please people.

Dammit, they need to form a map of hope
to help me find James.

Will the real slim poet please stand up?

Stand up and be heard.

I stagger in the darkness of my hidden
soul to find a purpose,

a reason, a sliver of truth in this sea
of self-lies.

But what if I find him, and I don't like
who he is?

Who I am?

Is he someone my father would be proud
of?

Would my mother still think he was her
little angel?

Is he an asshole?

Cause I'd just as soon stay lost if he's
an asshole.

I mean, the real, real me who I try to
find in my bed at

midnight when I'm alone and up

with my notebook and collection of hope
slices.

Is he worth the pain?

Worth saving from the clutches of death?

Oh, James, be someone I could love
without shame.

It's like a plea I'd give a lover on our
way out to eat.

What if he's ugly?

Or weak? Could I deal with that?

What if,

what if he's a…woman???

Come on, I'm serious!

What if he's a girl trapped in my male
body?

Could I run fast enough, get lost quick
enough,

forget about my find soon enough?

What if he's dead?

Got tired of waiting to be found,

brought to light, or accepted, and died
in the vast

darkness of my collective being?

Do I live on?

Or do I die then and there?

Aside from the what-ifs, can I love
myself no matter what,

no matter what, no matter what?

I recently found another sliver of
light,

and it's the one you see in my notebook
now.

And it's a big piece of the puzzle,

previously hidden, undiscovered,

something I know to be true now.

I'm bisexual.

Dammit, I knew it!

I've accepted it.

But all these slivers of light in my
notebook,

what if they're pieces of James?

Have I been finding him in bits and
pieces of light,

and capturing them in my notebook?

Yes, wow, I think I have.

I'm not entirely lost then,

just been broken apart and forgotten.

Piece by piece, poem by poem, day by
day,

I've been slowly but surely,

finding James.

The real James, who had been shattered
by hate,

Now being put back together with love.

And a notebook.

And I love him.

I accept him.

I can save him.

I can honestly be him,

because after all,

I am him.

Bones.

My sincere apologies.

You have fallen, I'm afraid, in love
with broken bones, which can only repay
in dust.

What's left of them bowing before you,
they are too weak to follow orders, too
rigid to entertain.

They grimly stand at your feet, awaiting
any requests, although they cannot
follow through.

The skin has been taken, the organs
melted away, and even the heart has
decayed by now.

Deteriorating with every move, the dust
piling up at bony feet, only these old
bones are left.

Standing useless, prostrated by the cruel fractures and breaks of life, and the disease which has ravaged them so far.

They are what is left of a death sentence handed down from doctor to patient, like a grim heirloom of mortality.

They may be suitable for some sort of morbid wind-chime, clanking together with hollow thuds every time a breeze blows.

The powder they make may be a suitable aphrodisiac, like elephant tusks, and may help you or another in ways they could never help their master.

Maybe you can string them up and make a bone marionette, a puppet to play with, a metaphor of what has been, and sadly, still is.

But they cannot remain your servant, as they are quite useless and can no longer succumb to your every whim.

And please, do not place them in the dark closet in an attempt to be rid of a way to deal with them.

They'll clank together something awful, like something out of a ghost story, and you won't be able to sleep.

What's left of the skull, smiles at you for eternity, or at least until he loses his jaw. Perhaps they can aid in the magic spell of some witch, some potion, some boiling cauldron in need of lonely bones.

I see you cling to them tightly, not wanting what remains of the remains to remain anything other than yours.

Look at them, how they emulate Shakespeare, holding the skull just so, and posing dramatically; what a card!

They want only to serve you, entertain you, be next to you.

They refused even the grave, not wanting to lie in a pine box waiting to become dust.

The dust that has accumulated already, you store in a small wooden box.

How curious, that you rub it on your skin, and sprinkle a bit on your pillow, almost like you were a woman Death dated.

Your love remains constant, while your mind seems to be ever fading.

You cannot be serious, the event would be a travesty, like a wedding mixed with a funeral.

You cannot get married to a pile of bones!

Oh, listen to me, I sound like your mother on the day before that first wedding of yours!

Anyway, those bones are no more fit to be husband of any sort, as you are to be a wife to what is left of a skeleton.

For God's sakes, tie them on the back of the car, like cans, and drag them along when you get married to a real man!

But no, look at you, putting each piece of bone in its place, lining them up the way you think he went, on the honeymoon bed.

Once again, I say, you cannot be serious!

These bones are certainly not going to do the trick, this is an exercise in sheer futility.

If he was barren and dry before, he certainly is no different now.

But here you go, turning off the lights, playing with the skull, holding a crumbling hand, teasing old bones that cannot fulfill.

Another metaphor snaps into place, a useless, bony man who cannot fulfill, a woman who is out of her mind, and a narrator watching from above that no one heeds.

It's like three years ago, all over again!

Well, at least this time, you can't do any more damage to him than what's already been done.

All you can do at this point is, make twisted Death get a hard on, and grind that skeleton into a fine powder.

My sincere apologies.

You have fallen in love with broken bones, which can only repay in dust.

What's left of them awkwardly sprawled
underneath you, they are too weak to
follow orders, too rigid to entertain.

Or maybe, just rigid enough.

Enjoy.

Signs.

I can see the signs in paper lines,
And the ink in my pen waits and pines,
To dot my poetry with inkblot stars,
And make constellations within stanza
bars.

Create a universe of paper and ink,
Where who you are is what you think,
And imagination mixes with the pain of
being,
And one hides behind the other for a
double meaning.

Recycle this paper by planting my words,
In the hearts and minds of those who
have heard.
Then burn my page in effigy,
And plant a seed to replace the tree.

Replace the ink in the pen with my own instead,

And see what lyric incantations can be written in red.

Summon me an angel to bless it all with a kiss,

And curse me if my ignorance has been written as bliss.

Then fly, my Christian Phoebus, and spread it to all,

Who wish to hear truth, and be changed, and stand tall.

Go question authorities who worship glutton and vice,

Go proclaim that we end in neither fire nor ice.

Find one who has a third eye to interpret the signs,

To see beyond metaphor and read between the lines.

To see the blood on the page crying out to be read,

To avenge the wronged innocent, and the innocent dead.

To trace my constellations of figures
unknown,

A new cosmos, zodiac, horoscope of my
own.

Hidden within written poetry, these
signs beg, understand,

You are more than an animal, more than a
man.

You are stardust transfigured by
creation's power,

You can shine, can create, but so short
is your hour.

Oh, I can see the signs, for I wrote
them for you,

Find a poem on a crumpled page, what do
you view?

You are reading the question in the
rhythm and rhyme,

But the answer lies before you in the
form of a sign.

Like the freckles that constellate your
face with countless zodiac,

The signs beg you look past the lines
written in black.

For your face I can see, and I hear what
you say,

But really, I am reading you in the most
intimate way.

So learn to interpret the signs that are
hidden,

And you'll be able to read the writer,
not just what is written.

Summon an angel to protect you from
society's claws,

For they will rip apart your poetry and
signs without pause.

And beg them to spread the word to those
open hearts and minds,

It is for you faithful readers that I
write these poems, and signs.

Infiltration Warning.

You are becoming infiltrated by the
message you are reading,

and with this page, your mind is mine,
for a time.

If you continue further now, it means I
am succeeding,

you are feeding off of these words,
simply because they are in rhyme.

For rhythm and rhyme entangle you, you
become enthralled,

even if you stopped reading it now, the
message is still in your head.

So remember not to believe everything
you read, or you will fall,

for by following even that advice,
aren't you believing what you've read?

Be wary of poetry that draws you in to
phase you out,

or to get you to believe all the lies
they like to tell.

Don't be victim to words power, listen
to what they are about,

so that you will not fall victim to
rhyme and rhythm's spell.

Remember this message, and ask questions
before you start believing,

so that you can be keen to the tricks of
rhyme magicians.

For you truly are becoming infiltrated
by the message you're reading,

but lucky for you, evil pursuits are not
this word wizard's ambition.

This is your Infiltration Warning.

Voice of a Fighter.

I'm fighting this sadness,

and slipping into madness

so deep in my psyche that I barely
escaped out of it.

I'm reminded of times when I cried over
dying,

the only thing I could do was suck it up
and keep fighting

for my life and now, this strife wants
to destroy it over bullshit, well fuck
this!

I'm not gonna let it rob me of this
gift,

given to me by god cause he knew just
how hard it would be to be me

in this harsh society.

Disabled and weak, but I'm able to
speak,

so watch out for me, I just might shock
you into believing that a

cripple can do these things so
eloquently, despite surgeries,

divorce, and pain, of course,

so bad that I think if it ever ends, I will cease to be,

so please just see me for my poetry, and not for these complications.

That's not how I see myself, why should anyone else?

Can I run fast? No.

Can I work? No.

Can I lift heavy objects? No.

Can I write poetry? Hell yeah!

I can put a poem together so passionate that you'll not only cry,

but think about why, and when you're done thinking about it,

you'll become passionate too.

A poem so powerful you feel charged and ready to do whatever

you have to make your dreams come true too.

Spin words together so beautifully that they are more incredible together than apart,

I'll make them like they belong together,

blend together like the colors in a Picasso hanging high on the walls of my mind.

Cause I love art, music, poetry, free-expression. I love the feeling I get when I'm at a

slam and the other poets' words just consume me like a raging fire, electrify me like I

was plugged in, and inspire me to write more deeply,

beautifully, provocatively, wonderfully.

Because I, I am not the sum of my broken parts!

I'm a writer of poetry and song,

a contributing patron of the arts, and the heart,

and don't you think for one goddamn second

that any doctor telling me,

"He won't make it past 25," is gonna stop me.

See, it didn't stop me when I was 18 and they didn't think I'd live that long.

I'm here, I'm Bear the Poet, and I'm forever strong,

until my dying day and god I pray and
hope that it is far away

because I have much to do and share with
you.

I've got to escape the madness and
sadness of my own life, it's true.

I'm crazy, baby, occasionally, maybe,
but it keeps things in perspective when
I flip back

to being sane because the game of life
is not to win or even love, or even
live,

it is to do those things as if you had
one day to share your gift.

Because with passion, you can love like
a poet, you can live like a legend,

and you can even win like a true
champion,

But without it, the madness, the
sadness, will overtake you again.

See, I'll beat it this time, but next
time, I'll dive in.

And you can bet your asses, I'll live to
tell about it!

Because I am a poet, a lover, a writer,

and mine is a voice of an overcomer, a
believer, and a fighter!

Scars.

These scars are my own,

made from the pain

that I have felt alone

and counted gain.

I have much been

ripped apart and then,

healed and ripped all apart again.

I wear with pride

what took tears and time

to heal and feel

so real inside.

My heart is broken,

shattered, open,

and bleeding.

the scar outside it isn't the one that's
healing.

I am steadily rising

to the top of my horizon,

and I will never decide

to give up and just die

or forget,

about the scars that it took to get
there,

where I will finally catch air

underneath the wings that are spread out
waiting to carry

me,

to the pinnacle of history,

cause this story

is one that my scars will tell of me.

But more importantly

than the scars, inside or out,

are the ones who are my healers,

my believers with no doubts

that I can make it,

and take and break the prejudiced ways

of the world which wounds us all,

every single day,

when we fall.

So I pray that my scars will never fade
away,

they stand as a grim testament to my
passion and pain,

my sacrifice and love for life, my
counting loss as gain.

They will stay where they are,

even the ones on my heart,

to heal others whom the world

has hurled

and ripped all apart.

A constant inspiration to dedication,

and patience,

a virtue that we need much more of in
this nation,

so wear your scars proudly,

cry loudly,

if you must,

cause when the weary and wounded

need acceptance, it'll be us.

We will comfort the fallen,

and heal each other on the way,

until that one day

when all pain shall go away,

when all tears are wiped for the final
time,

so enjoy your scars, although they make
you cry,

and pity your enemies who gave you your
scars and pain,

for it is they who will feel all the guilt and the shame,

and when at last, the healer comes to set us free,

they'll be left behind to be scarred eternally.

Forever ripped apart, forgotten and denied,

their scars will never heal, while ours will give us pride

and life, and love like we've never ever felt,

cause scars are power in heaven,

and only pain, in hell.

The scars that our dear Lord faithfully endured were just as painful as ours, and just as real,

but the one thing we can all be assured, is that by His stripes we are healed!

Gerald.

(Legacy of Dust.)

This is not a poem I would like to write.

I have never written about you before, I have never wanted to.

This is the first poem, and maybe the last.

I know your name, your number, even where you live.

But I do not know you at all.

I am unsure as to if I want to, but for the first time, I will write about you.

Can I say it?

Can I even mouth the words?

I am the son of a coward.

I knew nothing of you until long after my dad died, the one who adopted me.

The one who raised me.

I think about what I would say to you, should I ever attempt to contact you.

How would I go about it?

It would be the very definition of an awkward conversation.

I think about going under false
pretenses, as a survey taker or
something.

But then, I would only be showing my
darker heritage, like the dark side of
the moon

coming to light.

I have no pictures of you, only the
story.

That while I was fighting for life, and
losing, as a baby on life support, you
left.

That you were once married to mom, this
was hidden from me until this year.

That you were a volunteer firefighter
for Legion Field.

And I ask myself, can a firefighter be a
coward too?

I know your name, but they are only
words to me.

I know you have another son, a Jr.

I don't know exactly why you left, other
than you didn't want the burden of
fatherhood to

a sick baby.

I think about my burden, a rare bone disease that can only be genetically passed from

the paternal side.

A disease that causes them to slowly deteriorate, until nothing but dust is left.

You left me a legacy of dust.

But I say to you, like a phoenix from the ashes of death and despair, I rose.

I have been through seven surgeries, countless doctors, needles, diagnoses.

I am supposed to be dead, at least 3 times over.

I am not supposed to be walking.

I am not supposed to be here, now.

I am here for a reason.

You were but the means to an end.

But I am the means to a beginning.

I will die trying to get into English books.

I will not die until my own is completed.

I will leave a legacy of love and bravery.

I will not stop writing until my hands are dust.

And I just want you to know, you're not worth the paper this poem is printed on.

That I did it without you, and I defied my heritage of cowardice and shame.

That I will be synonymous with other great names:

Shakespeare, Whitman, Dickinson, Eliot, Neruda, Gibran, Hemmingway, Faulkner,

Cummings, Frost, Joyce, Hughes, Roethke, Berryman, Plath, Ginsberg, and Smith!

These men and women, and so many others are my family.

I read many of them while in hospital beds and I read them still today.

And I want you to know that what you left behind is indeed greater than the sum of his

broken parts.

What you left behind was a child destined to be ahead of his time.

And I don't know if I'll ever meet you, I'm certainly brave enough to try.

But do I want to?

Not now, maybe someday.

Could I forgive you?

Could I ever possibly forgive this?

I'm certainly brave enough to try.

But you will never know me, you have missed out.

Gary, my dad, died a hero, and taught me all he could.

He is my father.

You are nothing but a name and a story.

And in the end, the only thing you'll ever be remembered for, if they remember you at

all, is not what you left behind, but who, and why.

I did not want to write this poem, but I did.

Because believe it or not, I adopted a legacy of bravery from the one who adopted me.

I may not know what you look like, but I know what you are.

You are a coward, and you failed the test.

I have the true voice of a fighter; I bear the scars, especially the one you gave me.

But you are a footnote in an empty book.

I am the writer eternal, and the books
are mine to write.

Now, don't you wish you stuck around?

It doesn't matter.

I don't.

I reject your legacy of dust.

I turned it into a golden pen.

A pen that will never have to write this
poem ever again.

The Cleansing.

White feet sink into the water.

Careful hands grasping the tub, as hips
ease in.

Sitting and laying back, you sigh,
adjusting to the warm water.

You don't need soap for this cleansing,
only water.

You don't need a rag to scrub the dirt
and filth away from yourself.

You don't need anything to lather in
your hair, your fingers travel thru
tangled terrain.

You stretch and your eyes find
themselves on the door.

Checking the lock, you make sure you're
safe, alone, undisturbed.

No one else needs to know of this
cleansing.

You run your hands down slowly, to your
submerged feet,

then back up, tracing every inch of
skin.

You think of masturbating, but decide
against it.

This night needs to stay pure.

They find your belly, breasts, neck, and stop at the head.

You gingerly slide down into the water, until your nose is an island.

You take a breath, and sink fully underneath.

Your eyes open, a watery naked world greets them, you smile.

You test your lungs, holding your breath until the very last second.

You arise gasping, dripping, grinning.

Once more, you find yourself underwater,

this time moving around like a giant in an undersea cave.

Your hand stretches up alone, reaches down for the cord.

Underwater, you hear the muted din of your mother's old hairdryer.

It reminds you of her, how she always used to mess your hair up with it after fixing hers.

You smile, and close your eyes to enjoy the memory.

It's the only memory of you and her that doesn't need cleansing, the only pure thoughts.

You open your eyes smiling, ready to be free and clean again, as it drops.

White is the last color you see, an assurance of the purity that's always escaped you,

and the ultimate sign of a cleansing.

Countdown.

He is a wounded shadow, hiding in midnight's gentle arms.

Tonight, he makes his bed on grass and darkness.

He lies on his back, staring at stars.

His eyes reflect glowing orange streetlights.

He breathes like the tide rolls.

A storm brews inside him.

He misses her badly.

Moonlight reflects tears.

He sighs.

Runaway.

She stands high on a lonely ledge somewhere, crying, afraid.

A betrayed soul wanting to end it all now.

She stands on trembling feet, as tears roll.

She feels the rush of wind blowing.

She hates what she has done.

Voices call to stop her.

It is too late.

She plummets below.

She dies.

Suicide.

He walks a hidden path to town, finding a church.

From a distance, he already sees the growing crowd.

Coming for food and shelter, he finds sadness.

He pushes through the crowd, invisible again.

He hears voices tell of suicide.

He looks up, seeing police.

And below, a body.

So much blood.

He cries.

Sister.

I am Called by the Stars.

I am called by the stars,
which are eternally there,
to rise to their heights,
beyond this earthly air.

To shine like a sun
to those trapped in my pull,
and to give life and love
to these orbiting jewels.

To burn brightly in spite
of the vast darkness 'round;
To glow red hot or white,
bright enough to be found

By that one searching eye
who might happen to see
the glow of my life,
and be inspired by me.

I am called by the moon
to reflect God's bright power,
His grace, love and truth,
to the darkest of towers.

To glow like the King,
a much smaller amount,
for I'm only a wasteland being
flung about in space without

His choice to have me to spin
'round the one who needs me most;
those in darkness without Him
now have me as a host.

When only blackness is there,
my dim light guides the way,
and reflects the star of all prayers,
who guides us through our day.

I am called by the earth,
to give life to the weak;
To protect those who hurt,

and give love to the meek.

To let oceans of my tears
be the lifeblood of all,
for unless healing occurs here,
every living thing would fall.

To rotate 'round the source
of my life and my light,
and to respect the force
which divides day and night.

To be fertile and giving
to those whom, on me, depend;
To be a father to orphans of living,
and to the lonely, a friend.

I am called by the cosmos,
to respect God's power and might;
To realize the Lord of Hosts
brought this universe to life.

To be as vast in my knowledge,
as I am devoid of all hate;
To, in black holes, take solace
that such is not our fate.

For we were placed on this planet,
with the right recipe for life,
so don't take His design for granted,
else we face eternal night.

Yea, I'll answer the call
to fall on my knees and humbly cry,
"My God, You made me and made all!
Without You, what am I?"

UNI VERSE.

Molecular universe suddenly flung
Between the paused and heavy space,
Resting between the speaking tongue,
And the look posed upon the speaker's
face.

The eyes, they well, and tears do fall,
As a frown is formed where once a grin
Was shaped by the news of the talk,
The tiny planets and stars, they swirl
and spin.

The space between two words of grief,
So sad that one would break a heart,
Occupies the tiny universe of its untold
speech,
And holds its future in trembling lips
barely parted.

Suns generate and stars explode as ever
so slowly,

Words, they come to life, so heavy with
the pain,

The pain of the speech, that they
simply, totally

Hold its balance in a moment's time.

Worlds collide and smash; galaxies
rotate and spin,

As the second word is on the verge,

The grief-stricken phrase about to
begin,

Causes the creation of human souls, as
stars merge.

And the soul of man, smaller than an
atom,

Begins to develop speech of its own,

Slowly but surely, leading to Adam,

Who wonders who he is, why he's alone.

Upon discovering his universe,

He finds he's only a speck, an intricate
part

Of a grander plan, a steeper curve,

Thus, these created souls develop heart.

Intelligence formed, theory questioned,

And pretty soon, a society, a government,

A world, a galaxy, a universe grand,

And who is the creator of all this?

Theology, mythology, the God discussion,

Beliefs on how their universe came to suddenly be,

Leading to the church, a great percussion,

A dent in the state just beginning to see.

Morality, ethics, rules and laws,

A world created within the universe

Formed molecular when a grief, briefed pause,

Comes to be, before a distressing word.

So, are we someone else's pause?

Our universe, their troubling secret,

And the universe created by us,

Creates more and more, universes
frequent.

Who are we, but a saddened stop

Brought on by tears of utmost emotion,

And our universe created by another's
thought,

Which spun everything into motion?

If this be true, the tell me this,

Which came first, speech or man?

A universe or a labored breath?

Are we not the ones from which all this
began?

Are we the gargantuan tongue or the
grain of sand?

The Last Conversation.

She sits at home,
talking to George,
even though she's alone.

He isn't there,
and I am unsure
that she's even aware.

Somewhere inside,
two lovers talk,
although one lover has died.

And one's staying on,
inside she walks,
although her legs are gone.

Look at her smile,
like he's sitting right there,
but its been quite awhile.

Happy but sad,

Without a care,

daydreaming until dead.

Now she leans back,

her eyes glaze over and shine,

but the smile doesn't lack.

She dreamed until gone,

George telling her inside,

"It's time to go home."

Unborn.

You are the moment that formed every
other moment before and after;

the womb of my destiny.

Unborn, I stretch the boundaries tight,
and kick within my skin, you feel me
seething.

Touch the most sacred place, I have been
there.

In the innermost caverns of your being,
so deep that you do not know you,

I am the hidden source which ripples out
your every move.

I am not your lover, I am a forgotten
part of you, screaming to be known.

I move my head, you cry; I speak poetry,
you fall out, speaking tongues.

You have given birth to any time I ever
was,

and given meaning to the places I have
been, before I knew them.

The fallible sun sets into the sea,
oblivion; it cannot bow any lower.

A supernova bursts within the formless
void, I smell smoke.

You take my hand, it crumbles into flesh.

Your fingers draw the line by which we measure horizons.

The world is not spinning; you're just that good of a dancer.

Life and death do not exist; only some being drowning in an infinite sea,

and you are the sailor who saves.

Humanity is the miscarriage of God, the unformed twin.

You clawed your way out, a survivor, gasping worlds for breath.

Time was the cord which connected you to God, ready to be cut.

Space was the fluid, sustaining you, but killing the other.

Countless star-filled universes flicker and fade; the rolling tides of afterbirth.

Existence is the dream of creation; you are the waking.

You are the western mystery on the lips of a fly.

Taking a Hit. (Addicted.)

Her eyes cut me deep, like a razor blade to the skin.

A single tear sheds much blood.

She looks away, my heart hurts.

This pain is my indulgence.

I need to heal, but she's an addiction I can't quit.

So every scar is sliced again, every wound is left open and festering.

She infects me with a disease I seek her out to suffer from.

I'm like that 60-year-old smoker who needs to quit, or he'll die, but is trapped by habit, and the urge to inhale cancer.

My urges are stronger, and her kind of disease is worse.

Am I masochistic?

Do I enjoy torture?

Well,

yes, and no.

I mean, c'mon.

Have you ever loved a woman?

I rest my case.

She shows a smile, glints at her fangs.

A serpent I would be willing to defy any god for.

A rush that's more powerful than any drug, but just as addicting.

Eyes I cannot crawl my sorry ass out of, like a deep blue well or pit.

And an ass I'd die slowly for, just to be able to sink my teeth into it.

Yea, I'm a biter, what of it?

I won't lie, she's a bitch at times, and if were walking outside in the cold, it's still not the month of May with her.

It's still cold as fuck, the only comfort is knowing that when we get inside, her pussy is

tropical, even on the days I'm not supposed to know.

Ah, those lips, they're worth every ounce of poison I must endure, worth the pain I so desperately need.

And her mouth ain't bad either.

Another set of lips I love.

Yeah, I said it.

So here I am, taking another hit, a drag, a needle, a smoke, a snort, a fuck, a slap, a bite, a tear, a cut.

Because that's what addicts do.

They get high, they get wasted, they have fun.

And they all die from it.

I'm only two lips, an ass, and another good fuck away from the grave.

She's taking me down with her, or vice versa.

But either way, I'm a dead man in love.

With a venomous bitch.

Yeah, I said it.

So bite me,

I like it like that.

Collisions.

You young people,

always crashing and smashing together.

Bumping, grinding,

pushing, pulling.

Colliding into each other

with your penises, vaginas,

breasts, hands,

wet mouths, nipples rock-hard,

little asses, legs sprawling,

tongues shoving, thrusting your hips...

I'll tell you one thing, my Mary and I
never crashed into each other.

It was all about the game of chase, and
playing hard to get, and flirting even.

It wasn't all about the payoff, payoff,
payoff.

The prize was made very special because
it was earned, and so hard to get.

And so worth it in the end.

My Mary and I never ever did all that
hot nasty mess, though.

Not even when the game was over and she was mine.

She's gone now, and I'm just here, waiting.

And you youngsters make me sick, make me sad.

You make my stomach turn.

The days of chase and woo are long gone, methinks.

And that, young man, is truly a tragedy.

Love ain't all about the sensual pleasures of the flesh, ya know.

Mary was too good, too wonderful to be treated like a piece of meat, like a, a tool!

And I won her heart by being a proper gentleman, and she won mine by being a lady.

A real lady, yes sir.

Not by dancin and struttin all sexual and nasty.

Dammit, you've ruined both the art of love and the art of dance!

You make love, you don't take love!

But the world has turned again and ground itself deeper into the pit.

Gotta keep your head up, boy, and your
heart in the right place,

out of the dirt.

So just remember, when you crash, there
is always at least one casualty.

See, Mary and I never ever just
collided, son.

We fell.

Numb.

Lonely summer nights,

Everybody else is fucking,

Everybody else is fucked,

Meanwhile broken poems don't write themselves.

Broken poet continues looking for the reset button on his life that doesn't exist.

All he can control is the channel and the volume.

I have a feeling down deep in my gut, telling me that the only reason some people keep fucking is to stop being so numb.

I choose to feel, even if it means pain, because in the end, I want to be remembered for loving someone, not just having sex with them.

Lonely summer nights spent adding to my pile of dust, another poem, another grain.

When it is all swept away, will you ever want to be clean again?

Dust goes on everything, and everything goes to dust.

You will be touched and changed, by a force you cannot feel.

Another numb body walks by, filthiest of all, but unable to change.

They pity my weakness, I pity their loss.

If they weren't so numb, they could feel my strength.

Lonely summer nights bleeding from your own blades, cutting to feel, fucking to feel, cutting and fucking everyone else because you figure they're just as numb.

Oh no, the nights aren't lonely for you, but they lack something vital.

I know what I lack, but are you even aware of what you're missing?

What you used to need and love?

I know you miss it, but you built up an immunity to the real thing, because it hurt so bad the first time.

Yet, now you need another pain to convince yourself you feel at all.

I know you miss the real thing, seeking it out, but unable to remember what it truly is, your only barometer is the physical connection.

And it's broken.

You could look love right in the eye,
not see it, feel it, or even care.

Just cut them all, fuck them all,
because if they're not already numb,
they will be soon.

I bleed from your reckless blade, and
feel the pain willingly.

Cut me all you want, I don't need it to
feel,

I need it as a reminder of what real
love is not.

You look at me, at us, but do you see?

You see only dust, and cannot feel its
touch.

Another lonely summer night, and
everyone is bleeding.

But can they feel the pain they ignore?

I feel my own, and yours too.

I'd rather be a broken poet than a
bleeding lover who has forgotten the
price of blood,

and only knows love as a sensation they
can barely feel anymore.

It is for you, the numb, that I prepare
this dust.

Boxes.

A chilling wind blows through the empty spaces between our walls.

The walls we built to keep us safe are trapping us within ourselves,

and we cannot escape delusion and artificiality.

Cold and numb, we stagger on in our dazes, in our own prisons.

Even the spaces between us are haunted.

Suffocating from our own air,

going crazy from our own four-walled existences,

and becoming blind from our own views, we fade to black.

The walls we built are closing in,

and the spaces between are thinning.

Boxed in and dying; welcome to America.

Land no longer free, and home of the grave.

Every day spent inside, we die a little more.

Without even knowing it, we build our own coffins,

and the spaces between only leave room

for the living to walk above and among the dead.

It's getting harder to tell which is which, these days.

The boxes of the living and the dead

brush by each other in the morning rush, and the mid-day meetings,

and the evening walks, and the nightmares.

Inside our enclosures, we stare ahead at the wall,

blindly, slowly pushing forward into oblivion, where, ironically, we're finally free.

Grave upon grave lies in field after field,

and chilling winds blow through the empty spaces in-between us;

in-between each and every sullen box.

FreeDOMINATION.

And tell me how far can you bend your
knee,

did they break your back,

do you feel oppressed?

And tell me how heavy is the weight
you're holding,

is it crushing you down,

do you need to rest?

And tell me why you bound those chains
to your feet,

those chains to your arms,

did you know they were chains?

And tell me those visions that they make
you see,

do they make you smile,

while they enslave your brain?

And tell me do you love your American
masters,

do you love their foot,

planted upon you as you cry out?

And tell me do you like being robbed daily,

seeing everything stolen,

don't you just wanna shout?

And tell me do you really know who to fear,

who destroyed the dream,

and told you who to blame?

And tell me do you feel safe in your cell,

in your box of lies,

or are you becoming afraid?

And tell me why you finger the key everyday,

and don't even know it,

because you chose all of this.

And tell me are you strong enough to break away,

from what they offer,

and refuse their enticing gifts?

And tell me when you are free and they hunt you down,

when they tempt you again,

will you be dragged back with them?

And tell me do you know what freedom truly is,

have you seen the light,

or are you fine with being dim?

And tell me in the end, can you pay the cost,

can you sacrifice,

all you hold dear for the truth?

And tell me do you know how many rights you have lost,

can you even talk,

or have they taken that too?

Rapist.

I have been raped.

Now, before you make your minds up about anything, know something:

This didn't happen last night, or last year even.

I didn't get wasted at a bar.

I didn't trip over anyone's dick.

I didn't feel anything until it was way too late.

Because this is not recent, this was more gradual.

Today I woke up and finally saw the bruises, saw the hole, felt the pain.

There's no need to call the cops,

and yes, you're the first person I came to.

So I'm guessing you want me to stand here and talk about it.

To go into detail.

To put myself on the spot and bear my soul.

Well, where should I begin?

We had always known each other,

I used to think he was my hero.

My refuge.

As I grew up, my eyes were opened to his true nature, but I didn't wanna leave.

Couldn't.

This could get long, so maybe I'll skip to the part where he started bragging about his purple-mounted majesty, or telling me about his rocket's red glare, and how his bombs were gonna burst in my hair.

He said he'd make my ass red, white and blue.

Oh, you know him too?

So you'll understand me when I tell you that I remember now.

I remember being bent over and fucked by the system.

I have been raped by politics in general.

I have been raped by a cold, calculating, ever-expanding government.

I have been raped by the greedy stock market.

I have been raped by big business and evil corporations.

I have been raped by the oil companies.

I have been raped by the federal reserve.

I have been raped by a half-assed, soulless, and apathetic fucking health-care system.

I have been raped by corrupt cops, officials and politicians.

I have been raped by a never-ending war machine.

I have been raped by Republicans, Democrats, and Independents.

I have been raped by a few cruel and senseless laws.

I have been raped by the unjust justice system.

The list goes on!

Now I ask you,

Don't you feel violated?

Don't you see the bruises?

Don't you remember the fear you felt when he pointed at you and told you, "I want you?"

When he bent you over with homeland insecurity, and you were powerless?

When he stuck that big USA missile up your ass and fucked you with it?

When he smacked you around with the insults of a criminal bureaucracy?

It's not, "In God We Trust" anymore.

It's "Oh God, We're Fucked!!!"

I remember now!

But I also remember him finishing up.

I remember him shouting as he came, "E Pluribus Mentula Unum!"

Out of many dicks, One.

I remember him finally, finally, pulling out of my devastated war zone,

and looking at me with that green all-seeing eye, as he told me, "You asked for it."

Why must we continue to consent to the robbing of our freedom?

Why must we give him our tired, our poor, our huddled masses yearning to breathe free, if he's just going to fuck them over too?

All men are created equal, and all men are equally fucked if we the people decide to continue our pursuit of happiness, without first asking our country what we can do for it.

He just looked me in the eye,

just the same way he looked at you,

and said,

"You asked for it."

Now I stand here asking you, did we?

Did we???

Because maybe,

just maybe,

WE DID!

Traitors.

That day, I stood, a traitor to my
heart,

For loving you, I had, myself, betrayed.

Unwise to forces ripping us apart,

I sought to change the winds that, in
me, raged.

From day to day, you plunged the spear
of hate,

deeper and deeper into this heart of
love.

And daily did you poison me, though I
ate,

for unbeknownst to me, my love was not
enough.

I suffered and died, and to Hell, my
soul reposed;

in Hell, I suffered and cried, but for
love's sake.

But somehow, out of such a grave, I
rose,

Somehow, I came to life, amazing grace!

How sweet the sound that saves me from myself,

and sweeter still the one saves me from you.

And still, I put you high upon my shelf,

my torturer, my captor, must I view?

But now has fallen, my pagan golden idol;

the worshipping of whom, I'd already paid the price.

The need for a new godking love was vital,

and so I shattered your blasphemous statue like ice.

And now, I, realizing that I'd saved myself from death,

must now fill that void with one I do not know.

I must find one who completes me, with each breath,

but for now, my idol be these words of woe.

O woe is he who returns to the blazing
fire!

He who looks back on the burning city of
sin.

He who loves the one who damned him to
the mire,

and idolizes still the one who so
betrayed him.

For he, is such a fool, that he knows
not,

the price he pays until it's paid in
full.

And when his unknown debt is collected,
he will rot,

rot with the one he loves that makes him
fool.

But myself, rising above the mire to
stand,

falling only once, and then rising once
more,

have I not all the more reason to depend

on the strength I found inside me, to
conquer?

And this strength, condensed in words,
shall save me thus,

as well as those who read these words of
strength.

And if I can make strong others, and let
them bust,

out of their mires, then I'll do so,
lest they sink.

No more self-betrayed, or burned by my
own fire,

I rise to fight the greater enemy
inside.

One who tempts me often, and chains me
to desires;

yes, I shall fight this evil till I've
died.

For the Devil, and his minions, try to
vanquish,

this same spirit which you feel in these
words of love.

But he shall be one day, destroyed in
raging anguish,

by the protector of my heart, my God
above.

Besides the Devil, I am my own worst
enemy,

and I fight myself daily, to ensure that
good prevails.

You were only the mire which clinged to
my feet,

the real enemy, besides Satan, is self-
betrayal.

Chant of The Abyss.

I feel a sudden emptiness,
My soul cries out.
I wander in my restlessness,
With feet of doubt.
My words become my memories,
My friends become my enemies,
The page, the only place that frees.
My soul cries out.
I wipe away my tears of pain,
But still, they flow.
All I've lost is more than I'll ever
gain
Or ever know.
How much I wasted in my youth!
All of my actions, so uncouth!
All of my lies, revealed by truth,
But still, they flow.
The eyes of God, they look away,
Yet, always see.
I know there is a price to pay,
For every deed.

I've sinned so much, I know He's cried,

I felt no pity when He died.

For this, my eyes could be struck blind,

Yet, always see.

I stand before my own demise,

I see my end.

There is no goal or waiting prize,

For tarnished men.

I know why it has come to this,

I'm standing on the precipice

Of the hungry, infinite abyss.

I see my end.

I'm falling into nothingness,

Forever alone.

All of my dreams have turned to mist,

Vanished and gone.

The void is eternally black,

No end to despair, a one-way track,

I reach for God, but His hand pulls
back.

Forever alone.

Remnant.

There is a river underneath this bustling city.

Flowing and ebbing, roaring and splashing.

There is no delta, there is no bottom.

It is a river of silent rage.

Some days, it flows without reason,

it roars without ending, it drowns without remorse.

I have forced my silent river of rage into a curved line of deception.

No piercing eyes, no furrowed brow,

no clenched fist, no obvious origin.

Just a thin curved line held in place by a desire to mold masks and hide monsters.

It flows, my rage, underneath this bustling city, and ever so often, rises from the bottom, and floods every street and sinks every hope.

My rage whispers to me like a moonlit river, horrible things, unspeakable things, so honest that I have to lie to myself to feel better about what I even think.

They say the mask is a protection, your defense against the outside world.

Mine protects all of you, from all of me.

It protects me from you too, but really, it acts as a border between us.

And the river splashes and runs over our borders, cracking our masks,

turning us into the people we try to hide from ourselves, into horrible people saying unspeakable things,

with no regard for consequences or humanity.

My levee is about to fucking break, and the nightmares that truly possess me and tear me to bits, are those that show me my true form.

And they want out.

My silent river of rage and despair wants to drown this city, submerge it and turn it into nothing but remnants of a once great thing, like the towers and steps that they found beneath the sea.

I am trying to hold back this surging river, but the sandbags of optimism and hope just aren't holding, and when it all falls down, the true truth will come out:

That I wanna pull you all down with me.

That I hate your fucking ugly masks and treasure my own.

That I laugh at the misfortunes of the innocent if I'm hurting or had a bad day.

That inside, I'm arrogant and weak, full of tricks and ways to trick you into liking me even after you've heard this bullshit poem.

That I have you all fooled because I fooled myself first.

That I have this little bag of tricks to make you feel sorry for me, and that all I really wanted all along was your undivided attention solely on me for no other reason than I'm a self-absorbed megalomaniac with a broken God complex, a passive-aggressive attitude, and a cynic's eye, all of which are slowly destroying this poet's heart, because I'm too weak to admit that I'm too weak!!!

The river floods the city with a rage no longer silent, and all of your respect and admiration and sympathy for me drown in it.

All you see of me now, is a remnant, a husk, a broken mask, an artifact, a disposable weak shell.

That's all that's left of this poet and his reputation now, all submerged and defeated.

And now I'll lie on the bottom for the rest of eternity,

forgotten, fallen, taken down by rage.

My only visitors now are those of you brave enough to spelunk down into my ruins and remains, to study what's left of this once great city, and to use my downfall as an example in your textbooks, of how not to build a poet or make a man.

My Monster.

(Tonight.)

Tonight, the rain was a blanket,

but I wasn't ready for bed quite yet.

I just wanted to wrap myself up in the covers,

and stay awake watching the cars pass.

Tonight, the wine was good,

and all the people were happy,

and as I sat, I remarked to myself on their many facades.

They are all like little figurine toys, maybe automatons,

who walked and talked to each other outside,

and appeared happy and accomplished.

But then the toys went inside the dark castle,

and you didn't see in, but you knew,

in there lived an entirely different creature.

I wear so many masks on a given night or day, I no longer know who I am,

or am assured of my place in the cosmos.

Tonight, I am a shape shifter.

But I'm also in hiding, from those eyes
of one who taught me well.

I did not study; I did not take the
test,

I went in my dark castle, and changed
into a monster,

and slept for hours.

I was ashamed in the light.

I avoided her; I knew I was giving up.

Tonight, my friends ask me how I am,

I tell them I am hanging in there, that
gets them by.

I am alluding to the truth, but they
don't get it.

Tonight, I am hanging by a thread over a
fire.

I am hanging by a rope above a stool,
inside.

In every lie, is an element of truth,
and my truth, no one must know.

I hide and browse books tonight,
wondering what I'd buy if I had the
money.

The little rooms full of books, these
are my sanctuary.

But I am unholy.

Tonight, the wind is warm for December,

and I blame it on the Alabama weather.

But it's an omen, I have been bad, I have grown selectively apathetic.

The Devil is close by, and his breath heats up the winter air.

Tonight, the rain is a blanket, thick, heavy, wet.

And I am cowering under the covers, hiding,

terrified of my own personal Hell.

Afraid that I've become too great a monster to save,

and now, Satan wants me for his army.

Tonight, I am fake and a face in the crowd,

fooling them all into thinking, "He's a good boy, and nice.

He has a gift. He is harmless. He is a miracle."

The only miracle is that after all my stories, lies and many excuses,

they still think this of me.

But I fool myself as well.

Tonight, I am silent mostly, and observant.

Ready with an excuse should I be confronted with truth by my teacher.

Armed with disarming tales and situations, my march is a skulk,

and my camouflage is normalcy, and I blend in well here.

Tonight, I plot my return to my warm safe dark cave.

Where I will return to myself, plan my next scheme of social interaction, and write a poem.

A poem, yes, a narrative of my monsters ways.

Tonight, I am torn.

Should I appear tomorrow and do my best at what I'm unprepared for?

Or stay inside, asleep, and let the disappointment of the kind poet facade grow,

only to feed the rage of the monster?

I am a creature of habit.

Tonight, I will go to sleep when I get home,

wrap myself in the blankets

of rain and covers of facades,

and pray once more,

to die in my sleep.

Maybe then, I can kill the beast inside,

before my mask shatters and everyone
sees it.

Maybe then, I can escape and hide
forever,

in the darkest castle of monsters there
ever was.

Tonight, I wait to dream alone, and hope
it shall never end, hope to never wake.

Because only in my dreams can I see and
remember,

the real, real me,

who is dying.

Walking Home.

Walking home, I felt a blast of wind,
like an invisible wall; like the tease
of a hurricane;

like God, being so mad at me he wanted
to punch me, had swung and somehow
missed.

Walking home, the moon hung bleeding in
the sky, like a betrayed lover,

like a tiny planet that had been
crucified, like the blood red eyes of a
God who was angry, tired of waiting,
like a bad omen on a cosmic scale.

Walking home, my tears ran hot and heavy
down my cheek, and leapt off,

like an old man leaps off of a bridge,
so tired of the world's cold deceit,

like Satan was tempting me to finally do
what I had dreamed of, or were they

nightmares?

Like the tears represented every grace
and mercy God ever gave me,

leaping off one by one, screaming as
they fell:

"Wasted on you! Taken advantage of!
Taken for granted! Forgotten!

I give up! Maybe-you-should-just-stop-stalling-and-give-up! Jump! Jump and die! "

Walking home, the weight of the world on my shoulders,

but constantly toppling and getting heavier;

like the world itself, and I were cursed Atlas; like everything I had ever put off or left undone was upon me all at once,

and every day I had to feel it; like that old Beatles tune, singing of my fate,

"Boy, you're gonna carry that weight, carry that weight for a long time! "

Walking home, the last thing on my mind was you; the first being that as soon as I got home,

I was really gonna piss God off, and drop all this weight.

I was gonna give up.

But I got to my door, and there you were, waiting.

The wind stopped, my tears ran dry, and the last drop of blood fell from the wounded moon, and I smiled, and you smiled.

And I thought, ok God, maybe I'll carry this weight just a bit farther, just a bit longer.

And guess what? Being with you, makes it not so heavy, like you were my morphine, saving me from all this pain,

while I walked slowly, step by step, down the daunting hospital hallways of my life, holding your hand.

Each step closer to that final door, each step forgiving me my wrongs, each step motivated by you: my morphine and my nurse.

And so, here I am, this impatient patient of life, just trying to get to that last door, of that last hallway, on my last leg.

After all, we're all on the same difficult journey, just different paths.

And we must all find that one person who makes the thorns bearable.

Because in the end, when you think about it, we are all just,

walking home.

The Rift.

I could feel the rift between us as we passed.

The deep unspoken chasm.

As deep as an inner cavern carved out by the falling of God's teardrop.

It's an unsettling feeling, this tension.

Between the ice rivers of indifference and the fiery volcanic lava that flares up inside, we are more than what we show.

More than neutral.

And at one point, we cease to don the masks we wear each day, and become them.

At one point, we are no longer the actors in the play of our lives, we become the costumes, the props, the very show itself.

So what happens when the show stops?

What happens when the masks crack and break?

What happens to us when we become a prop in someone else's production?

No purpose of our own.

Just a costume that someone special used to wear, now hanging in a dark closet with other broken dream suits, used-up props, and old cracked masks.

I could feel the stone grip of indifference as our eyes met.

We no longer cared as we used to, but inside, I hoped this apathy wouldn't last.

This was just a tear, a crack, a rift.

A tear in the costumes we were, a crack in the smiling masks, a rift between one scene of the show of our lives, and another.

But this was no intermission, more like an uneasy pause between heavy sentences of harsh dialogue.

And as we passed, time stopped for a moment, the show of our intermingled lives came to a pause, and our eyes flashed the hate masking our love.

Because there was a rift between our hate and our love, they mixed, and one briefly overcame the other, appearing in our eyes a false emotion.

But what happens if the rift, the crack, the tear never fully closes, and over time, hate slowly mixes with and poisons our love?

Then what do we show?

The masks of our lives are cracked,

and we see the hideous monster beneath the painted smile.

The costumes of our lives are torn, and beneath the purple, green, and gold fabric of royalty, we see the soul of the hungry pauper underneath.

The unsettling pause between the glamorous and witty dialogue of our shows, gives the real meaning of the production away with a chilling subtext completely contrary to the show's dialogue and message.

So now, you see what I mean when I say,

I could feel, literally feel, the rift between us; like running my finger across the cracks and tears of the masks and costumes of our lives.

And it has never fully closed, and now our love and hate are mixed into some terrible emotion that we don't even know how to deal with.

I see what is underneath us.

And it is not all love, and it is not all hate.

It is simply a rift, which has given way to enormous indifference.

Therefore, this show must not go on.

This mask, this costume, this prop that has become our lives,

should be deemed useless and placed in the closet of forgotten dreams.

Unless we can become something else entirely: our true selves.

Able to break, but able to heal,

able to hate, but able to love,

able to lie, but willing to speak truth.

For if the truth can set you free, then does not a lie trap us?

Does not our hate tear at us?

And aren't our cracks and tears and rifts just the result of rough transitions, unspoken truths, and hidden emotions?

For these things to completely heal, we need truth, time, and perseverance.

Oh, and love, let's not forget.

You know, the greatest playwright of all time once wrote a line in his play that said,

"To thine own self be true."

(Ironic, isn't it?)

Otherwise we become what we play at: a mask, a costume, a prop, a show.

And the rift develops.

So now, here I am, becoming an active agent of truth and love in my own life,

as I turn around and follow you into the kitchen.

I'll wrap my arms around you, and I'll tell you how I really feel.

I'll show you that I do love you.

Because healing this rift is gonna take time and patience,

and I want to feel real, I want to be myself around you.

I could feel the rift between us when we passed in the hall,

but we didn't go our separate ways, and now I feel it getting smaller.

The cracks and tears of our lives, which leak hate into love and produce indifference, are under construction, in repair, and on the road to recovery.

The show of our lives is no longer a show, it's just our lives.

And those closeted broken hearts and dreams are now being carried into the light,

and either allowed to die or brought back to life.

This rift will not be the end of us.

On the contrary, it shall be the beginning of our true lives,

like the rift that opens up to give new life, then closes again.

That new life will face a series of rifts, openings and closings, tears and repairs,

from the rift of the open womb to the rift of the grave that opens to swallow our bodies and then closes again, the final rift.

This love of ours has been torn to give birth to a new life for both of us.

No longer a false show, our lives became a nursery for true potential.

We welcomed the birth of truth in our lives, and we bid farewell to the tears and cracks that separated us with indifference.

I hold you in my arms, my true, true love.

A love no rift can destroy,

as long as this love is not for show.

Shows over.

Healing complete.

Rift closed.

I love you.

The Rising.

Glory taken from pain in drops of blood,

There is strength in the weeping, and power in the flood.

The wound is open and the pain, surreal,

But we know of realest life from the worst of what we feel.

We rise, blood dripping, slowly at first,

Our tears streaming down will quench our thirst.

Our breathing is labored, and the muscles quake,

We fall again, and on the ground, we shake.

But we focus our energies on the glory ahead,

We steady weak knees, and raise our throbbing heads.

We rise once more, and trembling, stand,

Each step in blood, a testament to man;

But more so, the strength to even stand
on this sod,

is a living testament to the love of
God.

Bleeding without fear, weeping without
shame,

We step boldly, towards the glory we
claim.

But what we seek in glory, we've already
found,

When we rose once more from the
bloodstained ground.

When we choose to rise, despite blood or
tears,

We dispel all weakness, pain, or fears.

And thus, exude glory in each steadfast
step,

And inspire strength to those who have
not risen yet.

For our wounds shall heal, and our tears
shall dry,

When we refuse to yield, or give up and
die.

We become what we seek in the act of finding,

That glory is taken from pain, but it is found in the rising.

Facing the Storm, Loving the Rain.

The air, radiant with sunshine,
stirred by wind and heavy with moisture
blows through my hair like the gust
that tatters the flag.
Brings with it a sense of freedom, life,
promise, and ever-changing ways.
Takes from me, my tears, as they dry
in the wind, takes my shackles of heavy
thought
and makes them a feather to play with.
Blows my frown into a smile, and my
worry into joyous abandon.
I smell rain, the good kind, and I feel
the wetness in the wind.
This rain will clean us, purge us, free
us, nourish us,
drench us, refresh us, and yeah, it may
still sting
a little. And so I stand waiting for
this quietly emerging
storm to rise and blow my inner storm
away, drown it in a cleansing rain, and
bring with it

change, possibility and power.

The power to face the storms brewing in my life, in the future, and now.

Bring on the rain, I'll face this storm, and my own as well,

until I'm ready to blow them away.

And stand proud in it un-moving like the flag.

that it batters and tatters and tears.

I'll get battered by my storms

but I'll still be there in the morning.

Standing tall, proud torn, but in one piece, dripping, drying, and waving.

I wave to the storm

as the clouds gather.

Yeah, I'll take it on.

I'll take all of them on.

But I won't just wave as I

stand, I'll fight it.

and twice as proud.

Because I'm further down my

road than a stationery flag.

And I face my storms, welcome my rain,

and appreciate the air, stirred by wind,

heavy with moisture, and ready, as I am, for change.

Envy the Dragonfly.

Don't take for granted, dragonfly,

The fact that you can fly so high.

Zipping over, ducking under,

Here you stray,

There you wander.

Free as free can be,

While grounded mortals envy

You, oh dragonfly, please don't forget
your wings,

Are marvelous, extraordinary things.

In a common world of human rules,

You make all of us look like fools,

How cruel to think that I,

Could envy you, dragonfly,

I simply desire one coveted wish,

And that, my friend, is nothing more
than this:

To soar, to flit, to daintily hum,

Above the walking human scum,

To fly so gracefully

With heavenly rainbow-tinted wings.

Try as I might, I stupidly fail,

To fly like you, so I stick to walking
my trail,

Knowing I'd sooner die,

If I were a dragonfly.

But for such flight, oh, it's a fair
trade,

And for a short while, I'd have it made.

A longer life I'd surely give,

Just for a short time, to live,

As he who can wonderfully fly,

Although the thought would make me cry,

To think It'd be over so soon.

But I'd be buzzing, flitting over the
moon,

But sooner, still, I die,

Nonetheless, I envy you, dragonfly.

Summer Cross.

Evening in summer floats by like notes gone blue, with a touch of fire.

Sat back today watching cog meet cog, and heard gears grind with a fatal consistency.

Everything is falling together, or just enough to fall apart before my eyes.

Summer night, wind blows upon sun-bleached skin, wet with human dew and moist anticipation.

Somebody, quick, give me a piano.

Don't know how to play, but tonight, the stars are lining up, and maybe I'll bang out a little truth in my idiot savantism.

At least hand me that cloud up there, I'll use it as a blanket to shroud me from all the frozen ambitions of the men around me.

Because some things, the sun just can't melt, baby.

Some things don't burn so easy.

I say give me a beat and I'll pound out a rhythm on this drum of mine too.

Sync up our harmonies tonight, because we're gonna need a band to beat the heat.

The cogs fall together, and form a broken heart, dammit, I knew it.

The sky turns a pale shade of shut the fuck up and just watch...

Trees blow in the wind, and I feel a delicious sense of dread.

Somebody's coming to reign on my parade...

Grab the tarp, and we'll cover our fragile self-esteem.

Gotta shield some things from the storm, because what we lost last time still hasn't blown back in.

Stretch out tonight and crucify my pride, and have a bottled water handy.

It's gonna get thirsty hangin' way up there, waitin' on God to save it.

Forsaking my screaming pride, I cast my eyes on the long line of tombs behind me, all of which I escaped at one point in time.

Three days my ass.

The sky bleeds a savior red in the mourning, and I wake up to screaming.

Somebody hand me a cigarette, I don't smoke, but I can sit here looking like a future cancer victim can't I?

I should be smoking by now, indeed, but my will is fireproof.

So glad this isn't about the usual give and take of a poet's mind.

So glad this isn't about anything in particular, I enjoy rambling when it's this brilliant…

Uh oh, looks like someone pulled my pride off of the cross, won't be long now till it's resurrected again.

Goddamned rapture my ass, I ain't going nowhere till I finish this fuckin' cigarette…

But I never will, huh?

Looking at the sky right now, is so cliché, so I peer into your eyes…

Cliché again, bring back the clouds…

Naw man, because I'm most glad, so glad, that this poem isn't about you for once…

For God's sakes, time to go straight-up Judas on your own pride, because this shit ain't about you…

But no matter what, the cogs still form
a broken heart, and I realize that's the
poet's

M.O.

Fuck cliché.

Because even though it's not about you,
all of this winds up being that way
anyway…

Even the crucifixion and the sky…

Ok, especially the crucifixion...

They Tell Me To Crawl.

they tell me to crawl,

when my legs are stone,

when my bed a rustling tomb,

when my bones grind like granite hands
across each other,

fretting in agony.

when my breath is short,

and i'm stabbed by invisible swords in
the side, back, and hips,

when the hips lock as if i wasn't
supposed to use them.

they tell me to crawl,

and while they sound like good things,

whatever they are,

the voices are low and ragged and
terrifying,

and i fear if i don't crawl,

they will leap out of the walls

like soldiers in wait,

and eat me down to my dying bones.

they scream at me to write,

in the middle of the night,

and they tell me to fight,

when i don't wanna fight.

when i can't breathe

they tell me to crawl,

i lay in a ball and i bawl

until all of them call, crawl! CRAWL!!!

i could have given up by now,

i really really wanted to,

but the instinct to breathe and to fight
is too deep,

so ingrained in my system,

my slightly altered dna

holds my mother's strength

from when she was in an explosion

that robbed her of beauty,

and the man sitting next to her

in the car when it exploded.

and there she was, in the burn ward,

face horribly disfigured and swollen,

and they had to use meat from her thigh
on her face.

and apparently something told her

to roll around in her wheelchair,

burned as she was,

in such unbearable pain as she was,

and check on the other burn patients

like she was a fucking doctor.

they forced her to smile when

her face was a horror story,

and they told her, tell jokes,

and they told her to fight

so i know why they come in the middle of
the night, and

they tell me that even rhyme is
tiresome, write!

write for your life, you are saving your
life,

and they tell me to crawl,

and to walk when i'm crying and to

give it my all if i am to avoid dying.

they tell me to crawl,

like i was a goddamn soldier

waiting behind battle lines hiding out
in a foxhole,

surrounded on all sides by disease and
pain.

i was gonna fucking hand my gun over to them,

and let them take me prisoner, or kill me.

it was gonna be done,

i was outnumbered anyway,

but nooooo,

they tell me to crawl,

these fucking asshole twisted angel shitbags,

and it's like now i have reinforcements,

but only it's all inside of me,

so i start going all rambo on their asses, one at a time.

i hate these fuckers but i hate myself more,

so why the FUCK ARE WE DOING THIS?

i was done

and these things,

these wretched things that wake me up

whispering, good, good,

now crawl some more,

i wanna fucking know how all of a sudden,

shit is getting done up there,

i mean wasn't your boss on holiday for
like A DECADE OR TWO????

now what, he's back and his new game
plan is to torture me now

with what i asked for stupidly when i
was seven?

help?

this is help?

making me do it?

you gave it to me,

you son of a bitch,

NOW GET DOWN IN THE TRENCHES WITH ME AND
FUCKING HELP ME YOURSELF!!!!

who are these angel/demon halfway
rejects?

tell them i wanna fucking speak to the
manager!

they tell me to crawl,

and they won't leave me alone

but they tell me somehow,

in small ways, i'm winning,

but i don't know.

and i'm warning you,

don't ask for help unless

you really mean it

because it's like he's some high school
guidance counselor,

telling me i gotta do the work myself if
i want help.

and i'm only fighting this hard to shut
them up,

and to show that pissant in the mirror

that i'm better than his quitter, stuck-
in-the-mirror sneering ass.

i'm crawling, and i'm above him!!!!

did you hear that, you fucking dicks,

i said I'M CRAWLING!!!!!

now shut the fuck up,

and let me watch tv.

lord knows i deserve a break today.

it's timed down to the minute,

you know, so i don't slack off.

How I Killed My Father.

I snuck gingerly one night
into his bedroom, as he slept,
and whispered a voodoo curse
into his ear.

I poured poison into his morning coffee
when he wasn't looking,
then asked him if he wanted more sugar.

I found his gun and loaded it,
pointed it at his head with shaking
hands,
and closed my eyes as I curled my
juvenile fingers.

I put a rattlesnake in his car, and
watched him
get bitten and keel over, full of venom.

Then, I woke up one morning,
ignorant and indifferent,

and I lied to his face for the umpteenth
time.

And I didn't tell him I loved him.

Then I watched him drive to work that
morning,

already planning my next betrayal...

Cardiac arrest in an 18-wheeler

was the perfect way for God to tell me

that I'd broken dad's heart for the last
time.

And that's how I killed my father.

I Dedicate Obscurity.

I dedicate obscurity
to every poet of fame.
The famous poet inside of me,
still has an unknown name.
For some, there is no open ear,
to hear their gorgeous song;
for others, a million hearts appear,
who've known theirs all along.
There are verses worth repeating
that have never been read,
yet a million eyes are reading
verses from poets long dead.
So I dedicate the great unknown
to those whom we all know.
There was a time they stood alone,
from that, their songs did grow.
The poet who is rich and glad,
is a poet of clichés.
The poet who's poor and sore and mad,
writes words that sting the days.
They don't sell out, or give in,

or write pretentious trash.

There is ne'er a poet who's true to the
pen,

who writes his songs for cash.

Fame is good, but glory

will stand the test of time.

I am writing my own story

in poetry, line by line.

I seek to be immortalized,

interpreted, explained.

My poetry's far too good to lie,

in order to gain fame.

I dedicate the nobodies

to the somebodies we see.

For everybody is somebody,

when they write good poetry.

So bring it on, and write, my son,

and do not spare the famed.

In fact, do not spare anyone

who gives you strife or shame.

The poet should never be censored,

he should write what he feels,

and if you tamper with our words,

they become no longer real.

At any rate, the famed are great,

if they have earned their prize,

and use their power and words of weight

for poetry, and not pride.

But, for those who have sold out,

the truth is plain to see:

That a poetic poser is worse, no doubt,

than a poet in obscurity.

For the latter is true, and better than
you,

and you ruin poetry for the rest.

So it's you I dedicate obscurity to;

go back home, and pass the test.

I hope you fail, your poetry is hell,

and you deserve to take the fall,

for there are better unknowns than you
could ever tell,

and I wish we didn't know you at all!

I Loved Someone Who Knew Not Love.

I loved someone who knew not love,
who only knew the sound,
that those in love sweetly make
to one another, whenever found.

They knew the coo and call of love,
yet never heard it cry,
or weep tears so many that it is
drowned,
and begging its owner to die.

I loved someone who had loved none,
like I, or my steadfast heart.
Who had never felt one crumble and
break,
and fade away, apart.

They had a heart waiting to break,
but never gave it away,
to one like I, who shatters souls,
with the words I write each day.

I pray they find a jaded one,
who helps them sound the call,
of cries, and sighs, and hard goodbyes,
and love that makes them bawl.

I hope the heart they so defend,
is shattered with a shove,
of gentle hand, and sweet demand,
so that they may know love.

For: Emily D.

Passionate Raging Beings Flung.

Passionate raging beings flung,
rag-doll spinning children laughing.
Vain ambitions condition the young,
answers formed before their asking.
Head-games played on battlefields
of days and nights and weekend fights.
A mental sword we sharply wield,
made real in the pens with which we
write.

Passionate raging beings cross,
in the bleak darkness of the world's
fate.
We wander about, so empty and lost,
deprived and drained due to anger and
hate.
Insignificant to all else but one
another,
universes within are created and
destroyed.
We are made, played, and faded, just
like our mothers

and fathers before us; a cycle of void.

Passionate raging beings spun,

around stages and pages and ages of
life,

and meanwhile, while death is having his
grim fun,

we wax mediocre, and rid boredom with
strife.

We kill to breathe, and bleed to die,

we love to hate, and work to play,

but the time has come for us to try

to settle down and live another way.

Passionate raging beings crash,

into one another, just to feel the
sting.

Our loves are brutal, our lives are
brash,

and in the end, searing pain is the only
feeling.

We must resolve ourselves to love,

love hard, love real, love with no
stage,

for this love is the thing that flings
us above

the darkness of being, or the passion of
rage.

O Thou Infernal Libertad.

O thou infernal libertad,

whose direction has much gone awry,

vigilant, thy keep an all-seeing eye,

upon the people thee controls from on

high.

O thou infernal libertad,

thy men are strong, but thy morals weak,

and flexible. Thou dost not speak,

of the peril thou inflicts on the meek.

O thou infernal libertad,

who supplies us once, and taxes thrice,

who gives us tools for every vice,

but for virtue, begs we pay a price.

O thou infernal libertad,

who poets love to put in verse,

and yet, above all, they have it worse;

thou givest them only grave and hearse.

O thou infernal libertad,

upon which God once blessed in vain,

He was betrayed, and thus gives her
pain,

so that by her own sword is she slain.

O thou infernal libertad,

who other countries flood with contempt;

thou darest profess thyself as heaven-
sent,

then hellishly invade them without
consent.

O thou infernal libertad,

who frightens her own, to ensure power,

who would fall if all were to strike
this hour,

but alas, we sleep and are thus
devoured.

O thou infernal libertad,

who waves her hand, and armies run

to fight controlled wars that cannot be
won,

and die in vain by blast and gun.

O thou infernal libertad,
who sickens us with virus and disease,
then brings her people to their knees,
by charging to rid each cough and
sneeze.

O thou infernal libertad,
whose obscenities are endless, day by
day,
but tells her people what they cannot
say;
ensnare the tongue, and the mind is
clay.

O thou infernal libertad,
whose myriad crimes are well-defined,
who frees the guilty, but the innocent,
binds,
who tilts the scale, and keeps Justice
blind.

O thou infernal libertad,

I write about thee whilst in my cage,

and so much more would I write, in my rage,

but thou chargest me for each pen and page.

O thou infernal libertad,

of thee, my verse shall madly tell,

if only t'were that in verse, you would dwell,

for then man would have his Heaven, without this Hell!

True Friend.

True friend.

You do not heal my wounds outright.

You open them wider so that I can see what must be done to heal myself.

You do not wipe my tears.

You tell me jokes so filthy, that my tears disappear, streaming down laugh lines.

You do not help me up.

You ask me if I tire of being walked on, and I am convinced to crawl until I can walk again.

You do not give me pep talks.

You kiss me and prove that love still exists, and I walk away talking to myself in amazement.

You do not reassure me when I am afraid.

You give me courage by reminding me of what I've already defeated, and I walk away feeling like a badass motherfucker.

You do not tell me I am a good poet.

You explore the hierarchy of landscapes, moods, and symbols in my poetry, and by extricating me, make me a better poet.

True friend.

Take the knife out of your own back, and slice me open with it.

For in wounding me with love, you heal yourself from the cuts of hate.

Let my blood and tears be a testament that real friendship hurts, it's difficult.

If we can't rip each other to pieces, really break each other's balls,

and then go drink root beer sodas while watching Scrubs together,

I have no use for you as a friend.

That's the real shit that friends are for.

Not the sappy shit, but the hard emotional shit.

True friend.

Who will piss me off with the truth, and then tell little white lies the rest of the day.

Who will call bullshit on me when I'm bullshitting, and read right through the mask everyone else sees.

Who will tell me when I'm being an arrogant asshole, and then brag about being the best friend a guy could have.

Who will surround me with people that might conflict with my mentality, so that I learn to use my voice when I need to.

True friend.

There is nothing more immortal, and yet more human, than you.

I would not live if not for you.

I would only exist.

Thank you.

Cancellation.

You tell me lies, I speak my truth.

We're trying to cancel each other out.

You wallow in your darkness, I spread my light.

We're trying to cancel each other out.

I'm disgusted by you, I love you.

You ignore me, you love me.

We're trying to cancel each other out.

You hide brokenness, I exude strength despite it.

We're trying to cancel each other out.

I need you, I don't want you.

You feed me, you don't satisfy me.

We're trying to cancel each other out.

Your death of the soul in spite of life of the body.

My life of the soul despite my death of the body.

We're trying to cancel each other out.

Your need for depth, my need for height.

Your living a fight, I'm fighting for life.

Your beauty exposed as superficiality.

My ugliness exposed as a need for pity.

We're trying to...

We're trying to...

We're trying to cancel each other out.

Your need for deception, my need for attention.

We're trying to cancel each other out.

And if we were to assimilate, oblivion's not far away.

We might find fullness in each others' abyss,

but instead we fight each other, wondering,

"Who does he think he is?"

"Who does she think she is?"

Why can't your subtraction and my addition

make at least a digit, a symbol, a power?

We're trying to cancel each other out,

and fading in the process.

You don't believe in me, I don't believe in you,

and cancellation of each other is all
that becomes of it.

We're trying to cancel each other out.

We're trying to cancel each other out!

WE'RE TRYING TO CANCEL EACH OTHER OUT!!!

And we're doing a damn good job!!!

Cosmik Politik.

A Parody.

The other day, the world blew up.

Angels flocked to God's side, where the Almighty was reading a book.

And sure, he had already read it in its entirety before even picking it up, but He was bored, so He read it our way.

The angels came in, "Oh Lord, terrible news! The world has blown up!!!! All of it!!!! It is as if someone had pushed the Armageddon button!!!

What shall we do? Did you know this would happen?"

God looks up from chuckling at some Richard Dawkins book, "Of course I knew."

The angels were frantic, "Well what shall we do?"

God flips a page, "We shall organize the souls of the good and the evil as we have always done."

"Oh my!" the angels cried, "was this Satan's work?"

God glances up, "Probably."

There is a long pause.

"I mean of course it is!!!" says God, saving face, "Oh my precious lost humans! I shall avenge thee, and Satan shall FEEL MY WRATH!!!!"

"Lord, he could be anywhere in the universe, where shall we look?" said the angels.

"Most likely hiding in some black hole. Send thousands upon ten thousands of my angels to every black hole in the universe. He will be brought to justice...eventually..." said the Creator as He returned to his book.

An eternity later, God floats on a cloud, giggling at Nietzsche.

Michael approaches.

"Sir, we have lost millions of our own kind, although thought to be indestructible, they were sucked into various black holes in space. We still have not found Satan, only a few of his minions."

God eyes Michael, "And what do they say?"

"They claim that their master was last seen talking to you, Oh Lord."

God vaporizes Nietzsche's scribblings. "Impossible! I would never be seen fraternizing with my greatest enemy!!!"

Michael weakly blurted out, "But Sir, what about that time with Job? You know, the cosmic betting pool, we all had money in the pot, Lord. Isn't that fraternizing with the enemy?"

"GABRIEL!!!"

Gabriel appears, exhausted. "What my Lord?"

"I am afraid Satan has got to one of my best, one of my own generals, Michael here. You know what we do to those who are fallen!!!"

"Yes but sir, now that Earth is gone, where should I put him?"

"HELL!!!"

Michael stammers in fear, "But God! I would never turn against you!!! Please don't do this, you cannot be serious!!!!"

Gabriel and the other angels drag Michael to Hell.

As they toss Michael in screaming, Satan emerges from the shadows.

"I hear He is looking for me..."

Gabriel, startled, replies, "Yes, and now we have found you, Satan!"

Satan holds an ancient and blackened finger up, "But before you say anything, I have a question. Why does he waste men seeking for me, when he knows where I am?"

"You are in Hell, as you belong."

"No, idiots, I followed you here from up there, I was hanging around in the back..."

"Trickster!" Gabe replied, "You are trying to confuse us!!! We are leaving!!!"

"As you wish, maggots, but ask Him something for me. Ask Him who helped Him push the button!"

Satan disappears.

Gabriel and the others return from Hell.

"We have done as you commanded, oh Lord! We saw Satan!!!"

God acts angry, "What? Well let's go get him and bring him to justice for killing my precious children!!!!!"

"But Lord," Gabe says, "Satan wants us to ask you, who helped you push the button????"

God turns around, expanding in size.

"GUARRRDS!!! Satan has tricked these too!!! Off they go!!!"

But before anything happens, more angels rush in from all corners of the universe.

"It's hopeless sir, we have lost more angels, and their deaths are in the trillions now! Wouldn't he have stayed around here or in Hell since he is most suited to this plane?"

"Do not question my authority, Ecanus, and do not forget your duty to seek out and exterminate this master of terror. This will be our final battle!!!"

"Sorry sir, it's just that without earth, nothing in your book here can come to fruition, only the defeating Satan part, so what is the point, oh Lord?"

"The point is not the battle between us at all," says Satan as he pops into view from nowhere. "The point is, Oh come on, Jehovah, tell them!!! It's all about souls in the end, we just cut things a bit short to speed up the game!!!"

"SATAAAAN!!!" yells God.

"Oh stop it, J, you don't call me that unless they are around. It's Lucifer, and cut the crap."

Ecanus, the angel of the writer, steps forward, and begins writing all of this down.

The other angels look about with shock, dismay and confusion over the two quarrelling like a married couple and not battling each other to oblivion.

Gabriel sneaks off to rescue Michael from Hell.

"Oh alright!" exclaims the Creator. "So I'm a bit of a gambler. I am afraid this too was all a bet."

God hangs his head.

"Pay up, sore loser," says the Devil, "I had more souls in the end than you did."

"So you two pushed the button together????" questions Ecanus, "No horsemen, no seals or scrolls??? No plagues or battles or anything??? Well that's no fun!!!!!"

"This is wrong!!!" exclaim the others, and they all start getting angry and agreeing with each other.

They get louder and louder.

God yells,
"EEEEENNNOOUUGGGHHHH!!!!!!!!!!!!" and
sucks the remaining angels into black
holes He spontaneously creates.

Only Gabriel and Michael are not
destroyed, as they were just now
returning from Hell.

Ecanus, in his final moments, throws his
scroll to Gabriel just before getting
sucked in.

God and the Devil turn around to see
Gabriel holding the scroll, and standing
with a very grateful Michael.

Michael speaks up, "So you two were in
cahoots the whole time??? You, (points
to God,) had me throw you, (points to
the Devil,) and a third of our kind down
to earth??? For a bet!!!??? For a
GAME????!!!!"

Gabriel concurs, "Ridiculous huh???"

God and Satan look at each other, then
back at the two remaining angels in the
universe.

God steps forth, "Hey, you two wanna
give the whole thing a try? Creating,
playing around, doing whatever, the
whole spiel???"

Gabriel replies, "But what about all those souls? Just make a new earth, and give them new bodies???"

"Yeah, make them look however, you can have this universe, while L and I go play with our new one. I have some cool new ideas. Instructions are written in the last scroll"

Michael blurts out, "I can't believe all of this led to here!!! And where the hell is Jesus???"

Lucifer, stepping on a cloud with God, replies in laughter, "Oh, he's around here, somewhere!!!"

Gabriel shouts out, "But how in all good conscience could we possibly do this??? How can we do this without you???"

God shouts out before disappearing, "You can do it! You just gotta have faith!!!"

The two dismayed angels look at each other, then at the scroll.

"So, should this be a part of their new holy doctrine when we create them?" asks Gabriel.

"Ah forget it. Well, I mean that can be your holy doctrine," says Michael.

Gabriel puts his head in his hands and sighs, "You wanna be the bad guy, don't you???"

Michael replies, "Just for an eon or so, I have always wanted to give cosmic villainy a try."

The scene fades to black as the two Archangels, and future foes, walk arm in arm, off to create a whole new world to destroy...

The End.

Love Insight.

As I look into your eyes,

I observe the dissolution of time.

I see the cataclysms that commenced humanity.

I see the cataclysms that will eventually annihilate humanity.

You touch me: a cold chill, a hot flash, a warm feeling.

It's as if you control my weather, my storms, my shining, my partly cloudy temperament.

You can forecast my whole week and calm the hurricanes inside me.

They hardly ever reach shore anymore...

In your iris, I see the cycles of life and death, the journey of the hero, the processes of the earth, the outer ring of the hidden heart.

I want to traverse your dusty roads, your bright and lively city streets, lie down in your desert and gaze at the stars of your conscious being, fireflies dancing in and out of your oblivion.

I swim your deepest oceans, find peace in your regenerative forests, find terror in your sudden natural disasters: the tornado of your parent's divorce, the tidal wave of emotion over your father's death, the wildfires of anger over being discarded.

I want to calm your storms the way you calm mine, but some storms, you just have to let pass and hold on to something strong for a while.

Some tears can be prevented, but some must fall to water the soul and induce a growth from the inside.

I escape your whirling eye, ever spinning, ever busied by a worried mind.

You stare deep into mine now, and by your looks of dismay, I know you've found my demons.

This is the greatest intimacy you could ever give me, knowing me well enough to see what my demons are, accepting the fact that I even have them, and loving me enough to help me defeat them entirely.

You walked up to each and every one of my demons: the demon of arrogance, the demon of melancholy, the demon of past wounds, the demon of jealousy, the demon of self-pity, the demon of procrastination, the demon of bottled anger, the demon of endless trickery…and you tamed them with unconditional love.

You escaped my iris of pain and empty promises, and you kissed me like I was about to leave you forever.

You held me so tight I couldn't leave if I wanted to.

You lay with me and slid your little ivory arm about my hip, and told me I had nothing to fear anymore.

I turned around from viewing my box of illusions, and told you, "But I still have fears. My biggest fear is losing you in the course of time. I wanna go when you go."

You looked at me and smiled, a single tear tracing its way down the lines of a face I knew by heart.

You told me "Don't worry baby, I'll leave you something to remember me by," and your wry smile was suggestive and endearing.

Ah, I thought, but you already have.

We conversed in bed until we grew tired, and just before hitting the lights, we just lay there giving time no mind, entering each other via the open windows of the soul.

I stared into you, you stared into me.

We battled each other's dragons, calmed stormy seas and did away with lists of worries, fears, and what-ifs.

We are changing one other just by being there, just by understanding each other, by grabbing the other's hand and saying, "I will go where you go, be more than a companion, but counterpart to the other's heart, and by understanding you, in turn, unravel myself."

Your eyes, your love, they do amazing things for me every day:

They save me from myself.

They love me for who I am, not who I could become.

They hurt when I hurt, smile when I smile, do what I cannot.

And in the end, as the life cycle carries us to our final task, we will look into one another's eyes, and create and destroy our final universe, battle the final dragon, who carries the sun in his mouth, and succumb to the final darkness while dancing in the light of our shared love and trust.

This time there will be no escape from that wonderful place inside the other, and we wouldn't have it any other way, as we weather the final cataclysmic storm, together.

Split-Stone Soul.

split-stone soul,
breaking through,
grinding bone against dry blood,
hammering until the crack of thunder
signaled a break in the rock.
split-stone soul,
aching to pulsate and beat,
waiting to crumble away,
and become more than reality can give.
cold hands grasp flesh,
scarred and weathered,
loving the hard way until
a break in the skin,
a drop runs free,
the blood no longer clotting,
the wound left festering, open,
the sounds of inner quaking,
as beats slowly return.
heaving mass of petrified flesh
breaking with each heartbeat,
opening and bleeding and not healing,

and finally feeling more than numb.

split-stone soul, be free,

split-stone soul, beat wildly,

and let our gods and lovers know,

we live once more, to love the hard
love.

we live again, real and pouring life.

we embrace the pain as a feeling,

and feel this split-stone soul,

beat and pulse once more,

bleeding in the cold and bitter morning
air,

free to die for the feeling of life.

free to die for the feeling of love.

freedom returns once more to you,

the hard and real and scarred to feel,

the split-stone soul.

I Keep My Promises.

I promised you I would bring you thru to
the other side,

but I never said you'd come out
unscarred,

I never said there wouldn't be barbed

wire ripping and tearing pieces of you
away,

scaring you with demons that I myself
put in your way.

See I'm God, son, I keep every one of my
promises,

unlike you humans with your bullshit
prayers and churches filled with empty
men,

see I never said you'd always win.

I never said that your heart would stay
unbroken,

I shatter to save, and I wound to open,

and son, I know you got your share of
scars already,

physically, mentally, emotionally, and
the pain is steady,

and every day when you clutch your
chest,

and you gasp for breath,

and you pray for death,

you just listen to this:

I WILL NOT GIVE IT TO YOU, JAMES,

but call my name,

it is Yahweh, YAHWEH!

You stand flayed, praying for a release
from the pain's flood,

but I have molded you with tears and
blood,

into the poet that you have become.

You see I promised you I'd pull you
thru,

you've been a permanent resident of
hospitals since before you were you,

and don't you know?

I see your scars,

I love them so,

I let those demons cut you so,

you must be cultivated to grow,

and so you must be half-destroyed,

cut, forgotten and then toyed with,

so that the poetry you spit

will heal others going thru this.

And when you cry out in the night,

shaking, breaking in your fright,

you say you can't see the light,

but my son, can't you feel the bite,

I send to your body broken?

An open invitation to the praise I want,
yet unspoken.

See, I want you awake, heaving,
breathing in pain so you

can write the messages that I want you
to,

see I promised I would bring you thru,

I never said I wouldn't hurt you,

I only said I would never desert you,

I've taken people, properties, and
material goods,

so that your broken heart would,

produce from pain, the power it should,

speaking words only I can speak thru
only you,

I do turn a blind eye when your faith is
untrue,

and hey, I DON'T GIVE A FUCK WHAT YOU
YELL AT THE SKY,

FOR I AM THE GREAT I AM,

AND I AM ON HIGH!

Holy, but also down below,

to hold your hand and tell you no,

NO, I WILL NOT LET YOU SLIDE THAT BLADE,

I WILL NOT LET YOU GIVE UP ON WHAT I'VE
MADE!

I will not stop the pain, my own son was
flayed,

and I betrayed,

and his dying cries were made

to break my heart,

so don't you FUCKING START

about fair and not fair!!!

I'm watching children die every day,

accepting souls that I prepared

for something else,

my creation wasted,

so have you yet tasted my agony?

It is the greatest pain to see me,

to be,

eye to eye

with the great I am,

so don't you damn me when I know you,

I made you,

I promised you I would bring you thru,

you beat death, and your breath is mine too.

Look around, son, you're alive,

despite the pain that I sent you,

to strengthen you,

so answer me this:

Did I bring you thru?

You're scarred, heartbroken,

and I have spoken

my truth,

and I don't have to fucking answer to you!

Just answer me, look around and answer me, are you

alive, are you well, are you happy too?

THEN SHUT THE FUCK UP ABOUT YOUR SCARS,

BECAUSE I DID,

I DID,

I DID BRING YOU THRU!!!

I Wanna Love You So Hard.

I wanna love you so hard that I break my
own heart and heal yours in the process.

I want to love you like that, break
myself to heal your wounds.

I wanna love you so hard my back breaks
from the weight of my heart,

and doctors advise me to let you go.

I wanna cling to you for dear love, and
forsake life.

I want to need you like air needs water,
like love needs pain in order to be
real.

I wanna lose the ability to walk because
it would cause so much stress to my
embattled heart,

that it would burst if I took another
step.

I wanna love you so hard my heart
fucking hates me for it.

I wanna love you so hard that my undying
love for you winds up killing me.

Alleyway Encounter.

Ambushed in the dark alleyway,
hands went on lovely hips,
and lips to hungry lips,
stretching us both to the tips,
clothes were pulled and ripped,
and thrown somewhere away.

Against the ivy wall I pressed,
and we began to begin,
you gently entered in,
and we made love there and then,
reveling in the sweet sin,
in the darkness, both undressed.

You whispered something in my ear,
I quickly turned myself around,
and then gladly slid on down,
beholding a scepter about to crown,
and finished you off without a sound,
and then we dressed and disappeared.

The New Godhead.

I split open the Godhead with my staff,
and its Abyss poured out like wine.
I took a sip, and let the rest splash,
then returned to hammering the divine.

The opened Godhead split wider still,
and the Rock of Ages tumbled down.
I swallowed the Rock whole until,
my stomach made a splashing sound.

I sought the Muse in Abysmal waters,
but alas, there was nothing yet there.
I set to find the Godhead's daughter,
and broke my staff making the final
tear.

I reached a trembling forearm in,
to the center of the most divine.
I did not fret about human sin,
for I am God's, and He is mine.

A clench, a tug, a frantic pull,
and with my hand, a hand emerged.
I yanked her further until, in full,
she escaped the gaping wound of father.

The Rock of Ages, steeped in time,
still made my fearful innards quake,
and so, I drank the Abyss as wine,
and thought the Rock my bread to take.

A maddening communion, followed by
rescue,
of Muse from Godhead, royally broken.
She cleaned herself of primordial goo,
and naked, stood before me, open.

I saw my beloved Goddess before me,
and instead of worship, fell in love.
The distant Godhead that always abhorred
me,
was cleft to birth the one from above.

Divine passion sparked, among Abyss,

before the Godhead broken by man.
I did not wait for time, in me, to pass,
I took her then, as was my plan.

My broken staff, the Written Word,
was the only way to open the God.
And as the Rock inside me churned,
we procreated on the Abyss-wet sod.

Oh Muse, my Goddess above all,
freed from ritual, religion, and
divinity,
has there ever been so sweet a fall,
than yours from Godhead, down to me?

We made love, as time passed still
lower,
and the Abyss, primeval afterbirth,
wrapped round the broken staff, my
tower,
and with the Word, conceived a new
universe.

The Godhead angered, but with fatal
wound,

was shaking as immortality became

mortal as man, and would die soon,

and the divine died raging out my name.

Oh, there are no priests or churches
now,

every soul is freed to follow her.

And as time festers in my bowels,

I rock with the Muse, upon the dirt.

Oh, seeds released, and spirits as well!

A new Godhead is being made inside.

I become ruler of heaven and hell,

and needing neither, toss both to the
side.

I ride, I ride the Muse electric!

Divinity plunged by the poet mortal.

No linear time, no measure metric,

and the earth, not destination, but
portal.

Time slips out, a pebble weathered by
man,

though before, man slipped out,
weathered by time.

The roles reversed, divinity descends,

gods become mortal, men become divine.

The Abyss encircles the new world made,

as a poet-centric universe.

The pregnant Muse is Goddess and God
displayed,

and my body fades, as I merge with her.

Man swallows time, and drinks Abyss,

taking both out of the Godhead broken.

The staff is the Word, broken from the
hits,

and man pulls Muse from the wound he
opened.

The poet births the Muse from the
Godhead,

and makes love to the unreachable
divine.

Then from the Muse is born the new poet,

and the universe becomes his to design.

Called Him Comrade, But He Was More.

I called him comrade, but he was more.

He was the hand upon my hand, the soul
interconnected with mine.

He was a lover and a friend,

my partner, and the company I parted
with at day's end,

for fear of rumors proving true.

I ate with him, and walked the shore
with him, beside and belonging to him.

There was no night he left my thoughts,
nor day he did not enter in.

And though my name was highly praised
among the halls of learned men and
women,

it meant more within even his few
complaints, and especially his laughter,

and in his sighs, my name rested
contently, knowing no other place so
well.

And in my old age, were he to be but a
memory,

and no more than the earth I've become
so accustomed to,

I will miss my comrade, but know where
to find him always:

in the dusty fields, in the open sea,

in the cry of birds, in the babble of
infants,

in the grass underfoot, trampled and
adored,

in the grey skies above me, in the
republic to which I also belong.

I know in these and more, he shall find
a home,

but no greater home can he enter in,
than that of my heart,

to whom he has given these songs.

He shall be remembered by others, as my
good comrade, and friend,

but to me, he shall always be known as
mate eternal, and lover true,

and even more than all of these things.

For Walt.

Brutally Honest Interview.

Yes, I admit I am obsessed with myself.

No, I don't need an intervention.

No, I don't think therapy would help, I can't afford it anyway.

Yes, my arrogance has been known to annoy people.

Yes, at times I completely change moods, and hate myself to the point of depression and self-loathing sometimes.

Yes, I have been known to sleep too much, and yes, I have been known to favor sleeping pills.

No, I am not addicted to anything, except taking pictures of myself, poetry, fat chicks, and family guy.

Yes, I have been known to purposely forgo my prescribed medications, either to punish myself, or because I would like to feel normal every once in a while.

Yes, I have used my disability to my advantage before.

No, I don't think I'm beautiful per se, but I do admit pure unadulterated brilliance.

Yes, I think I channel the great dead poets.

Yes, I am also obsessed with suicide, and the link between creativity and madness.

No, I am not suicidal. Anymore.

Wait.

Hang on, can you do me a favor, miss?

Can we switch seats real quick?

I'm sorry, I just realized there's a mirror behind me.

Ok, now slide over a little to the right.

That's better.

Thanks, now where were we?

FAT CHICKS.

I am here to confess something.

Most of you already know,

so I guess it's more of a declaration of intimate dependence.

It comes as no surprise to my guys and girls,

but for you newbies, let me curl your ear,

to tell you what I want you all to hear!

I LOVE FAT CHICKS!!!

I wanna swim in a river of jello-bellies,

and fuck my way out of an ocean of cellulite!

I must reiterate,

I FUCKING LOVE FAT CHICKS!!!

The low self-esteem,

the unassuming clothes,

as if you didn't know what the fuck you were doing in the bedroom...

That ass!!!

When I die, I wanna come back as a hand,

just so I can feel your ass jiggle when I smack it!!!

I mean DAMN!

I hate that these toothpick skinny women are who

society deems as the beautiful ones, the models,

the cheerleaders, the main characters…

I believe the saying that "real women have curves,"

and I wanna be the one to find every single one of them,

mapping them out on your body like a cartographer.

X marks the spot, now if I can juuust find that X….

Oh well, it's fun just trying!

Now, I'm not into circus fat, because let's be honest, too much is too much.

I want the buffet, not the whole damn restaurant!

And if SHE does, then you know it's too much…

I mean, if you're into that, more power to ya,

but bbw's, look out, cause I wanna do ya!

Wait, I mean, take the time to love you properly, the right way.

I'm the man with a slow hand, and half the fun is the foreplay!

Big girls are sweet, and love to eat, and I love watching them devour meat.

Pun intended, I admit, but just look at them!

They can shake it on the dance floor like no other women.

More boobs than you can handle, more handles than you can hold,

and no gal can light a candle to a big girl on a pole!

Got junk in the trunk, though that ain't no trash,

I'd dumpster dive all night if it contained that ass!

Fat chicks, I love you, and I'll ever be true.

I'll be your toothpick if it means getting inside of you,

WHOOOOA NELLY!

Slow down, Bear, behave!

But just look at that belly,

I mean she really takes the cake!

No, I mean, she literally just took the fucking cake,

and the pie, and the whipped cream, and the cherry too.

Pile it on, and eat up, hun, I'll crank one out while you do!

Damn son, save some for when you get her in bed,

Cause we'll be rockin and rollin until we break off the legs!

And I'm sorry I'm so blunt, babe, I'm just filled with such zest,

I'm so excited, girl got cellulite! FAT CHICKS ARE THE BEST!!!

The Flower.

it was always the flower i focused on.

it didn't save me from the pain,

it didn't make everything alright,

it was just a focal point to get me
through the whippings.

something to concentrate on as i
screamed and cried,

trying my damndest not to twist in pain,
because that made him angrier.

and if i even tried to turn around and
look him in the eye, there would be
blood.

very soon, i'll have enough spare change
collected for a bus ticket.

if i'm going to run away, i'd damn sure
better do it right the first time,

because knowing him, there would never
be a second.

i didn't do anything wrong.

i keep telling myself that, but in the
back of my mind,

i can't help but wonder why else this
would be happening to me if i didn't do
something.

a friend of mine once told me about this thing,

reincarnation.

says if you're good you get to be something better.

i want to be an eagle.

says if you're bad, you are reborn into a life worse than yours.

so i must have been a real bastard before.

but at least back then, whoever i must have been, i was better off.

i must deserve this for something.

i must have killed someone before, the way i see it.

then the belt cracks against itself and i snap to from my daydreaming.

he says i daydream too much, that i don't involve myself enough in this world.

says in this world, i am worthless.

but what do i do to become better?

to make sure that after he kills me, i don't wake up like him.

yea, i know, seems like a better place to be than mine,

with all that power, but i can tell
something tortures him.

tortures him like he tortures me.

but still, he is in a worse life than
mine, because he does not have a soul,

so how can god save him?

i may be covered in bruises, but the
good book says i can be saved.

it says the meek shall inherit the
earth.

that's because they are good people,
they will have better lives later on,

they will rise up and inherit the whole
mess.

i just want peace.

i just want a piece of land with my name
on it,

with a yard full of flowers.

i can remember a time when the flowers
on my bedsheet were soaked in blood.

that's the only thing i remember about
those days,

other than the pain, and the feeling of
blood running down my legs.

and the screaming.

it gets worse if you scream, but how can you not?

you hurt so bad, you scream, he beats you more, you scream louder.

i think that's what they call a vicious cycle.

vicious.

like a dog is vicious.

like my dad is vicious.

i remember the day my mother fell down that flight of stairs.

she died a day later.

he says it was an accident, but he doesn't know i saw him.

that was vicious.

so to keep from screaming when he beats me for

speaking out of turn, or looking at him funny,

or just getting caught crying in my room,

i pick the stained flower,

a flower stained with my blood,

and i focus.

i grit my teeth and i even bite my
tongue.

pain to distract from pain.

blood to distract from blood.

i thought about writing jesus loves you
in tiny tiny letters on that flower.

he would kill me for that, so i put the
words in my head on the flower.

jesus loves you.

he bled too,

he screamed and suffered.

his mother also watched helplessly as he
cried.

his father also turned his back on him.

i wonder if jesus had a past life.

but i know he didn't, he was perfect,
and they were afraid of him.

you can't get that high on the ladder of
reincarnation.

he was the one, the flower among the
weeds.

he was the focal point for the entire
suffering human race.

he died.

i want to die, but if i do it myself, i'll go to hell, or worse, wake up like him.

i don't think he's the devil.

i should.

he is just a weed who is angry because he could never be a flower.

weeds choke flowers.

they kill flowers.

does that mean i'm a flower?

i don't know, but if i am, my petals are withering, and i am in a place with no water.

my mother loved flowers.

she also used to love him, but i don't know why.

he beat on her too sometimes.

she kept promising me that we would get out.

he found out that she was going to have a friend of hers pick us up in the night.

two days later, i watched from my cracked bedroom door,

picking at the scabs on my legs, as he pushed her down the stairs into oblivion.

oblivion, my old teacher said meant nothing.

i love how it sounds in my mouth.

i used to wanna be something, now i think the only way out is to be nothing.

to dive into oblivion with mom.

he already is nothing, but he can't go where we're going.

we're going up.

we are climbing the ladder to better lives.

we are focusing on jesus and on flowers,

and on becoming something more than we were.

i don't find any peace focusing on that flower,

even when i put jesus loves you on it in my head.

but later, when i look at it, i think of how much like jesus i really am.

jesus came back after being dead three days.

he rose like a flower.

and the weeds could do nothing.

does that mean that in order to get out, i have to die?

three days is a long time.

but i'll do it just to get out of one day here,

where the only flowers that grow are on my bedsheets.

and the only words of love are the ones in my head.

i hope i get out.

i should hate that bedsheet but when i leave, if i leave, i'm taking it with me.

it will be a reminder of a bad past life, and the good life i had to focus on to get out.

if he kills me, i hope he wraps my bloody body in that sheet and buries me.

i'll rise up out of the ground, and be the only flower there.

i'll look at the weed who is my father.

and i'll say the only words i'll remember, from all the painful years of focus.

"jesus loves you."

Tower of Babble.

Babble, babble, babble,

I can't understand the words you speak.

Babble, babble, babble,

Build a tower to the god you seek.

Babble, babble, babble,

Heaven, Valhalla, Olympus' peak.

Babble, babble, babble,

God lives within the foreign cheek.

Babble, babble, babble,

Your languages are dead and gone.

Babble, babble, babble,

The words I say contain my home.

Babble, babble, babble,

The spoken word: God and Heaven in one.

Babble, babble, babble,

We all come together, we Babble-on.

I Have No Epic To Tell You.

i have no epic to tell you.

all the prophets are dead, their
prophecies have come true and blended in
with modern life,

teetering on the end of the world.

all the poets reserved to stages inside
their own minds,

their words all sound the same, and so
much noise is ignored by even other
poets.

the romantics have been reserved to
greeting card companies and their corny
lines.

all the preachers and their
sensationalized faiths have been
abandoned for skepticism and doubt.

the writers are crammed in hovels typing
out somebody else's story,

wishing to bash their own heads in with
the computers.

the stars are drunk and fucking, puking
off tenth-floor balconies or lip
synching songs they didn't write.

the knights in shining armor have been stripped of their awards, and dulled down; now wearing dark shirts that say SECURITY, and guarding those who think themselves to be royalty.

the guardian angels have given up on us, talking about how stubborn and selfish we are, during their smoke breaks from cubicle work.

they have been resigned only to advise us in the way of telemarketing and timeshares.

buy now you stupid fuckers!

the dreamers have awakened only to hate the waking world,

and crave sleeping pills and muscle relaxers, only to find out that even in their dreaming, life is a nightmare.

the musicians are either paupers singing beauty into alleyways and street corners for change,

or whores with thousand dollar instruments and cheesy pop songs who seldom remember or miss their beginnings.

i have no song to sing.

i have no great masterpiece of change.

i have no work of art.

i have sought to be all of these things,

but there is no one who will listen or
see.

the page is empty.

the microphone abandoned.

the canvas is blank.

the tongue is silent.

the epic story is us.

and we are all we need, as the world
explodes and fades around us.

someone somewhere is starting it all
over again,

and all i wanna do is be with you as the
end sweeps over us, consuming all.

hold my hand, there's no need to leap.

we're all already falling.

i hope the coming new world stumbles
upon us.

the only real thing i knew back then,
may be the only thing that lasts.

take a gander at our corpses, and know
love.

carry on, ignore the rest.

take this dust, new world, and write
your epic anew.

Ode To Tortured Artist.

Ah, you tortured artist,

when will you learn?

You snap the whip across your own back,

and wait for the burn.

The massive blurring twisted hungry
world tortures you.

Infinity, and all of its transgressions,

throughout and without time immemorial,
tortures you.

The page you raped with your seed of
ink,

the white forever spoiled for demented
thoughts

you cannot contain; this tortures you.

People, loud, opinionated, selfish,
swarming, fighting,

fucking, birthing, dying all in vain,
they torture you!

And to write! Oh the indignities to be
suffered!

The therapy sessions you should have had
when instead,

you turned like an addict to that dusty composition notebook; you are sick!

You are suffering!

You need help!

And still, no intervention, goddammit no, let me wallow in the filth of my prison,

twisting, producing angelic cries from demonic contortions;

the ground is soaked with dirty blood -- -- why won't you die?!

The drunken madness of it all, a plethora of pills and orgies, alcohol and the occasional herb.

Healing my ass, you're just looking to escape and get high.

Meanwhile, excuse me, pardon me, but do you have a minute?

I seem to have written this, and why should you care?

Like a street minister peddling tracts of biased salvation to those they deem 'lost',

you wander thru life, leaving behind pages and pages of no gospel, no savior, no salvation, and no devil or god but yourself to exorcise;

and leave it in rhyme so the demons can dance to it!

And where was my mind?

Off in my own head composing sonnets to stars and sunrises, angry letters to god and family, and ultimatums to facaded friends.

You're stuck there now, aren't you?

Trapped inside your own head, either screaming to be let out, the horrors are too great!

Or getting comfy in the dark extra space your mind dares no longer occupy, like a tenet fearing the crazy man at the end of the hall.

(I hear screams and music emanating from that room at night! I think he's an eccentric rapist or killer savant!)

For God's sake man!

Your head is not a room with a view in an upstairs apartment with a pissed off landlord and a shitty fall-apart building!

You can't live there if you already inhabit the space!

Oh tortured soul, your poems to suicide go unheeded by their muse.

I told you before man, she's busy in California, she WILL NOT fuck you!

You don't own a gun or even enough willpower to stick your dick in her and fuck yourself into oblivion.

The ride that goes nowhere has the highest fee, the longest line, and the most twisted fucking operator.

Abyss is not your funhouse, artist, pay your toll and get out!

I am my own whipping boy!

I misbehave, I must be punished.

My body fails, it should rot today!

I have no effort, I don't contribute,

just grab that knife and bleed out your sins,

you walking cesspool of sickening brilliance and raw emotion!

Grow a pair, meet a girl, (or a boy,) and let them punish you!

The works that come forth hence will be wonderful and brilliant by design,

and miserable line by agonized line.

Pour me a drink, and share your stage.

I have a song to sing.

Ode To Fuck All!

Fuck the bawdy crowds!

Fuck the rotten children!

Fuck the dream and nightmare!

Fuck the waking world!

Fuck the fly and hornet!

Fuck your judgment.

Fuck reincarnation. (Shit returns as more shit.)

Fuck this interruption!

Fuck the cosmic scale of balance!

Fuck the coward fathers!

Fuck death and fuck returning!

Fuck all,

Fuck off,

Fuck me,

Fuck yourselves!

The torture is weighty and delicious and palpable and otherworldly.

He must be so brooding!

The depth is beautiful but deadly to experience.

Take your razor-blade poetry, get out,

take your indoctrination, I am the
dragon and the pit,

there will be no soliciting here,
loitering is permitted by the

talented only who have proven
themselves, and otherwise,

on rainy Thursdays in June by all else,

take your mouth, place it here, pay the
fee,

bend over, grit and grin, take it like a
woman, man,

and go!

The bard has wept,

the drunk has slept in,

the pen is vomiting in an alley.

My pain is my bride, and she's always on
the rag,

you are the rag, soak it up!

Day in, day out,

inspiration, motivation,

desperation, lamentation,

mix them and swallow.

Take this pill,

don't ever call me,

go home and bleed on a canvas,

you tortured soul,

despicable artist,

loathsome writer,

worthless drunk,

hopeless addict,

clueless poet.

Take your art and eat it,

throw up on an accomplished writer's
shoe,

and really get it all in there!

Tell him that's poetry, you sold out
dick,

and move on.

But please don't stop the torture, god,
man, people, self,

heroes, mind, heart, body.

Damn all love, the source of pain,

dip in the well,

write until your fingers bleed,

bleed until you're weak,

sleep it off, wake up,

get fucked, write drunk.

Torture me now God, as you see fit,

because for fuck's sake, my poetry still
sucks,

and I must not be doing it right...

Wounds.

if i close this wound,

i'll have nothing to write about.

if you make another,

i'll be a better poet.

healing begins when you feel your pain,

and appreciate it as a sign of your
existence.

loving someone is just opening wounds,

making new ones, closing old ones.

when will you see that love is a dance
between the wounded and the wounder?

when i look for love to end the pain,

it's like looking for a knife to heal
this cut.

brace yourself, it's coming,

because somebody loves you.

sure, they don't want you to hurt, but
you will.

and you don't want to hurt anyone, but
you do.

if i hurt you just enough to make you an
artist,

if i wound you just enough to keep you
alive,

if i break your heart to shatter your
illusions,

you may not like me, but you'll thank
me,

and you will know love.

hold this wound open,

and tell me i'll live.

because it's better than healing my
wounds,

only to reopen them under false
pretenses.

if i'm going to love you, i'm going to
do it right,

but when i hurt you, i guess you'll just
have to trust me.

i must love you an awful lot...

Revolution Starts With Me.

does it feel fucking good?

to elect yourself king with no other
consent,

condemn your enemies who won't repent?

execute the criminal that you designed,

watch with roman eyes as you destroy his
life?

does the power seep from his smoking
eyes,

and his jolting hands to your prideful
thighs,

and can you feel his energy around you

when he cries,

or are you just dead inside?

does your belief system correspond with
genocide?

does it justify the death you decry?

does your god say "well done,

my faithful son,

now continue killing the unfaithful
ones,"

or is there no room for deity
upon your throne?
you are god inside yourself,
his powers are your own.
i'm a lowly subject, suffering,
looking up and wondering,
why justice is in your governing,
what does it feel like to be king?
it must feel fucking amazing.

and will your rule last?
will your subjects obey?
will someone save us fast,
from your self-given authority?
will there be a usurper,
a revolution staged?
will i be asked to take part,
in an active change?
because i've watched and waited,
as those around me died,
i've looked into their eyes,
during their final cries,

and i have wondered when the time would
come,

for these kings to fall.

but why wait then for a hero?

why not risk it all?

i have nothing more to lose,

i do not fear his tyranny,

i stand, a dead man, and i choose,

because the revolution starts with me.

Writhe.

Have you ever writhed in love before?

As if love was pain, but you wanted
more?

Tumbling in the dirt, a heart's demise,

a passion fire burns our souls alive.

Rolling in the leaves,

unworthy tears to fall.

Why have I never loved like this,

or felt this love at all?

Love is lifeblood flowing, flammably,

waiting for the spark to consume the
body.

I have writhed and sobbed, twisted in
contortions,

felt life inside me throb, then felt its
abortion.

Have you begged for death to give you
life,

at the razor's edge of passion's knife?

Have you bled your drops of painful
submission?

Or felt your heart beating to escape its
prison?

Have you rolled and cried,

howled and died,

moaned and sighed,

screamed and writhed,

in love before?

If not, then what is your love for?

You have not loved without this pain,

so love, and die, and writhe again.

Bone Dry.

bone dry, that's how i want this sea.

i want to open the floodgates and let it empty.

i want the creatures that live in it to wither and die.

i want the stone cold sun shining darkness upon it to fall,

and roll away until it breaks.

i want all the gods inside me dead,

all the churches burned,

all the believers swept away.

i want the new desert to be my covenant with myself.

i tire of being full of useless emotions.

the seething rage that flares out of me like sunspots,

or vomit, i want it all gone.

i want to release the tension, and sleep empty for a while.

i don't know how my blood can stand it, being constantly on fire.

if the only way to keep from burning
alive is to turn the ocean into desert,

then what do i know of the world?

or have i been swimming in kerosene this
entire time?

bone dry, that's the way to go: logical,
distant, analytical, detached.

that way, i can't drown, not in a cold
desert.

but i could sure as hell try if i wanted
to.

Marianne.

She's running away while standing in
place,

the darkness hugs her face like a veil.

And the house is falling apart like an
animal

suddenly dropping bones on its way to an
oasis it'll never reach.

The emptiness wraps about her eyelids,

keeps them just open enough to see,

and just tired enough not to look.

She's been deaf to the false charade

of family compliments for years.

She isn't even there.

Her hands sleep like stones in wait,

ready to crumble at the slightest touch.

She's unattainable; her space is not
your space.

She is her own frozen, slowly spinning
galaxy.

Somewhere in her center, a supermassive black hole

lurks and swallows her alive, bit by tiny bit.

She can barely remember you,

her memory is rounding the singularity now.

She's not old, just being erased.

Not dead, just living in reverse.

The child inside her shouts, chained to guilt.

She never meant to ruin her mother's birthday.

She was only 7 years old then, when she accidentally

swept the cake from the table, lit candles and all.

She can still see the fingers pointing, and the small fire rising.

But the voices that once shouted at her are now dull and vague.

The wind passes over her, as if she were a stench

so foul that even it would not be carried with the breeze on its way to the coast.

She feels only dull heat, and is used to the cold.

She's been married before, after all.

The darkness kisses her with pity.

It weeps for her in purple brush strokes across a dying sky.

She fades with it, and sinks into a chair.

Somewhere, in the fires of some hell,

her mother calls to her for forgiveness, but is never heard.

Her eyes glaze over; a candle flickers.

The chair groans as she falls asleep.

Night closes her eyes, brimming with forgotten beauty.

The wind gives in, and gently touches her.

She is gone.

Tonight's No Good.

tonight's not a good night to talk,

i've been drinking and i'm way too
honest when i'm drunk.

i might call you a two-face and tell you
i love you in the same sentence.

i might let my resentment slip out
somehow, and break my polite mask.

we'll discuss this later when i can
pretend to care more convincingly.

i'm already too readable as it is.

i want no emotion invited to our private
party,

where you tell me things, true things
that i hate to hear.

my rage would probably act up, were it
present, but it's strictly forbidden.

the "truth" you spit at me is chewed and
malleable, like a wad of gum.

you get to bend the laws you set, like
god defying gravity.

your double standards piss me off, while
i have no standards whatsoever.

don't try and discuss things now,

i'd call you a bitch and the fight would
be on.

you'd leave upset and i'd call you names
while you were gone.

i have to have a clear head to choose
the words i say to you.

so tonight's no good, and tomorrow's
shot, i'll be drunk then too.

The Grand Poet.

i look at the star-filled sky above me,

and think that the universe is a poem
god is writing.

each star is a word we cannot
understand,

even our own sun means something, though
i don't know what.

word by word, star by star,

he is writing his poem out for us on the
pages of space and time.

and while we here, spinning, like to
complain that god is not with us,

or does not exist, or does not care,

i know that god truly must be a poet.

off in the far reaches of the universe,
scribbling furiously,

deep within his own creative madness.

the poet does not stop until he is done,
just ask us.

and not just far away, but near us too,

the words accumulate like snowflakes in
winter;

piling indecipherable and lovely among and above us.

we will not be able to read it all until we die.

we will spend all eternity marveling at his genius, at our arrogance,

at the masterpiece we were a part of.

we tiny little creatures on a one-in-a-million rock,

are spinning around a star that may mean any number of things.

for all we know, it's another exclamation point.

and maybe we are words too, and maybe i am wrong,

but what if two people who are meant to be together,

are two words that belong together?

maybe we are both his language, and his audience.

if i shout my poetry to the stars, what are they shouting back?

what am i shouting by existing?

what is god writing to us?

or are we the words he writes?

we are all stardust, after all.

we are all being written by the grand
poet.

Anthology.
(Someone's trying to be way too deep.)

Someone's trying to be way too deep.

I don't like the anthology I'm reading.

I find myself scanning over most of the poetry in it, occasionally finding a gem.

Most of the time though,

I just put the book down and think,

"So this is what's passing for poetry out there?

This is what's getting published?"

Not that I think I'm so much better.

Well, one or two of them, yeah, I could beat.

But it's all open to interpretation anyway, and it's not a competition.

But seriously, someone's trying way too hard to be deep, to be brilliant.

And maybe I'm guilty at times,

always trying to step my game up,

always trying to bedazzle crowds I'll never see.

Maybe I should take a break,

or maybe I SHOULD try to beat those poets who have made it in.

But like I said, it's not a competition.

Maybe I should compose my own anthology,

and let poets in that I know are good,

REALLY good.

"The Best American Poetry."

Who do they think they are?

They're good books and all,

but it's time for the real America to be seen.

I don't know all of it, but I know someone who knows more than me,

and bit by bit, poet by poet, we'll multiply and collect our stories.

I want to be giant in the literary world, yes.

But I am NOT SUCKING ANY DICK to get into an anthology, a review,

a magazine, or a book.

I don't care how much I might like that in theory,

it's the principle of the thing, dammit!

Out there, someone is trying to be way too deep than they are.

They want Bohemia, but are too rich to have known it.

They want culture, but are too elitist to allow it.

They want pain, well, I can give them pain,

but so can life, so I say go for it.

They want to be us, don't you see?

Not really, but that's how we do it, we live hard lives.

That's how we write great poetry.

The depth we achieve is because we live in the mud,

and bust our fucking asses.

Because we know the beauty of life by living it, pain and all.

"The Best American Poetry."

Maybe in cool little book-filled rooms, with menacing literary figures,

sitting there reading and selecting the next batch of poems that sound deep,

beautiful, brilliant.

But not so in actual America: where the poet is outcast, shunned, and mocked for his art; where if he doesn't perform well tonight, he doesn't eat; where we write poetry to keep us sane because the madness and hatred around us is stifling, and even if NO ONE EVER READS THE GODDAMN THING, WE HAVE SPOKEN OUR PEACE TO THE UNIVERSE, AND THUS FEEL BETTER!

Fuck depth, we live poetry.

And don't get me wrong, some of these poems in here ARE good.

But please try to find more of the real thing,

instead of some thing desperately trying to be real, like a literary Pinocchio.

How pretentious! You're a liar!

Someone's trying to be way too deep,

and as a writer of truly deep poetry, it pisses me off.

You can bet I'll be writing that down in my anthology.

We're currently accepting submissions.

Posers need not apply.

No Utopia.

And behold, I tire of this penniless
profession,

and I tire of pennies, and of the debt-
filled dollar.

I tire of this land, I want a land with
no gods,

no churches, no money,

no war and no government,

no falsehoods, no divisions,

no races, no classes,

no schools brainwashing our youth,

no network news for the masses,

no filters, no censors,

no duty to god,

no duty to country,

no country, no state,

no wealth, and no hate.

I want a land that is free,

where you're taught only what is real,

and there are no expectations.

You decide your own path,

and you carve out your own roads

on the maps we won't have.

And behold, this profession,

of intimate confession,

of turning pain into masterpieces of
great introspection,

should be paramount in my new world,

as with art, music, dance, literature
and the like.

But the need to be paid will be futile,
we won't need it.

There will be no government money
produced from thin air,

given value by its makers, with interest
and debt for all.

And no Jesus, well, that's simple, we
have that today,

but in my world we won't pretend that
he's real, just to keep people in line,

with the crosses they bear, hanging from
their necks as a sign of their slavery.

And all it ever meant really was an
allusion to the zodiac and stars,

and mythology lent its stories to the
creation of a savior.

There will be no return, because there was no arrival.

The church be damned and condemned,

and yes I will lose friends from this,

but my anarchy is silent, except when freed from my pen.

I want a world with no idols, no man-written "holy" bibles,

no weapons or ignorance, just the heart of a child.

And yes, you will abandon me,

exile me to far away.

You cling tight to your delusions,

but the illusion is falling away.

I tire of the illusions, and the blind faith you put in them.

I want a new land, and for this, you will lock me up,

and so only in my mind will this utopia be real.

But inside all of your minds, you still share my ordeal.

So I guess I'm no different, I'll just stay here inside myself, and enjoy my fantasy land, just like everyone else.

But at least I am honest about what I am and why.

But behold, I do tire of this world, of this lie.

Behold, there is no utopia anywhere,

but at least I can try.

One Thing Is For Certain.

when they say that he's brilliant, do
they know that he burns?

they say he's prolific, (well, he tosses
and turns.)

they tell him he's deep, he still can't
find himself.

he's beautiful and sweet, but he's going
through hell.

one thing is for certain, he's going to
hell.

they say his words have power, yet he's
so fucking weak.

they read him for hours, while he cries
himself asleep.

his book sales are on fire, and he just
wants escape.

they love how he inspires, but he's
trapped in his hate.

one thing is for certain, he's trapped
with his hate.

they love his brutal honesty, (he
honestly lies,)

they relate to his ranting, he just
pretends to be wise.

they read words of such wonder, and
meanwhile he's drunk.

his lofty thoughts they do ponder, but
his thoughts are all junk.

one thing is for certain, his thoughts
are all sunk.

he posts poems in the morning, while
hangovers abound.

he sleeps without warning, there he
cannot be found.

his fans wait for the next one, (what a
gullible lot!)

they know his words are a gun, and they
wait for the shot.

one thing is for certain, he waits for
the shot.

All Hell, Our Masters.

The dawn awakens with teeth.

Aires opens his eyes; our brutal king rises high.

The locks all clicked open, the Subjects we're freed to roam.

The Great Eye turned and observed with a million little eyes.

I cannot break these chains, chains that feed me, chains that ensure my survival.

The world is a bank.

The world is locked away and enforced.

Any visitors who may have traveled light years to get here,

will quickly notice the system, and turn around, bound for home again.

They tell us there are never any visitors.

And that there have never been visitors.

Food comes swiftly in trucks, and I take an apple

and retreat to let the pigs feast.

Poor swine.

Underneath dry skin, our chips gleam softly in our blood.

Do not proceed to dig it out.

Do NOT interfere.

Money is now a digit heavily guarded.

Media is the end-all-be-all voice of truth.

What they tell us is what we hear.

All we hear is all we need to hear.

If we want something badly enough, we WILL pray to The Great Eye,

our new God, and maybe it will be considered.

Anarchy has been removed.

Civil disobedience has been removed.

Dissenters have been removed.

Freethinkers have been removed.

Entire countries worth of men, women, children and animals have been removed.

We were made in a new image.

The Great Eye Am.

Even our genes worship them, their creators.

Cattle is now what we are.

Slaves, an entire generation of slaves.

Houses have become large locked cubicles with VERY little personal expression.

All traces of individuality in any form have been removed,

unless authorized by the High Court.

We are made specific to the jobs we have been intended for.

We work the same job for life.

Enforcers are stationed in every community.

They outnumber Subjects 2 to 1 now.

In the whole world.

Public congregation is heavily monitored, and seldom.

The seas are locked.

The skies are locked.

The roads are locked.

The communities are locked.

Permission must be granted before any Subject can travel or access anything locked.

The High Courts have recently ruled that suicide is allowed,

with authorization.

Subjects can also ask to be removed,

but some desire the privilege of doing it themselves.

They want one final free act.

Subjects must apply for a suicide permit, in order to be temporarily weaponized.

You are watched, and you must commit the act within hours of applying.

I ponder all of this as I eat my apple.

Application denied, they said.

They need to keep factory workers this year,

as there have been many unfortunate accidents.

An application for exile may also be applied for,

though it is a slower, much more painful death.

This is because all uninhabited areas of the world have been rendered toxic.

I have also applied for this, as well as removal, but it is futile now,

as I know the same thing will be said.

They need factory workers.

There is always the possibility of an accident at work.

I finish my apple.

Aires closes his eyes.

No more war should be considered a blessing,

but with all countries seized and locked down,

unified in slavery, who is there to fight, and why?

Certainly not our omnipotent, omniscient masters.

All hail The Great Eye!

All hail our masters!

All hell, our masters.

The Pit.

Bolted your mouth;
shut up and let your tears be demands.
You are the mask,
a face,
a shadow of man.
There is no God here,
no pretend to spare,
there is no air on Mars.
Space for rent,
and no one sent
to fill the vacancy
left by mythology.
Your god is a star,
that is no flattery,
listen to me:
YOUR
GOD
IS
A
STAR.
And I don't need your words,

or your faces for play.

The stage is ablaze,

the audience has gone away,

the curtains are burning.

All the world's inferno.

Open your hands,

no debt repaid,

you still owe me, man,

that comes out of your flesh, today.

Hung by your wrists;

just relax and enjoy

the chambers I gave you

to reverse all your joy.

And when sorrow's your bird,

can you let it fly free?

Can you let it exist without killing it?

What is your soul worth without the
darkness?

Nothing that light couldn't buy.

Stripped you naked of clothes;

I saw the dirt where it lies.

Your genitals do not lie,

but your feet tell a story.

Is your shame heavy and pouring,

like rain when it's boring?

No time to let it be,

it has been, and it's not letting me,

so say goodbye, mother mary,

close your eyes and just see.

Your audience of crows

has arrived for the show,

so don't flail around them,

they might want to peck at your skin.

There are four inches of regret where
your penis has been.

And a crow flies away with a nipple, I
fear.

Souvenirs! Souvenirs!

Get your nuts over here!

This chamber's in danger

of sounding quite queer!

Bled you dry;

the last step, you can cry.

You've been here for days

asking me for a window, you tried.

But there's nothing to see,

the bricks have blocked the willow tree,

and the sounds of the wind past the vast field of green.

Is the blood running down?

You find yourself on the edge

of "I'm about to drown,"

and "I'm teetering on the ledge."

Well, jump off and jump in,

the water is warm, and the ground wants more men.

The bloodletting is better,

the slower you go,

it gives the victim hope,

while his clock races backwards.

Welcome to the time machine,

your brain will set the date and time,

your body will pay the price.

Just flash that life before your eyes,

that joke you called a life.

You worshiped a delusion,

and my final conclusion

is to give you some assurance

by your slow contribution.

Can you tell me when you get there,

what is on the other side?

The others couldn't,

but that's not the reason they died.

So have you enjoyed the pit?

I rather find all of it

quite amusing, you little shit.

I make another slit,

can you hear yourself dripping

away in the darkness?

Am I coming off heartless?

But you're not really real,

so it's all very harmless.

Beg, scream, and howl if you can,

you are the mask,

a face,

a shadow of man.

Departure.

Goodbye father, goodbye son,
departing when you've not begun,
have your ticket when you reach the
gate.

Take this paper, take this pen,
and as you ride back home again,
write for me a song that I can play.

Excess baggage, left behind,
out of sight, and out of mind,
they will have him here at lost and
found.

Riding free, you paid no cost,
and karmically, the bus got lost,
your feet will never ever touch my
ground.

I was born, and I shall die,
in this layover that lasts all my life,

waiting on a bus that will never show.

He was a passenger, that was passing
thru,

who just dropped me off, before I could
coo,

he was late for his bus, and said he had
to go.

There Is A Beauty In Despair.

there is a beauty in despair that bliss
can never hold,

the fears, the tears, the sorrow near,
the sudden feeling of cold.

a snapshot of searing hopelessness, is
more profound than hope,

the fragility, the humility, the
inability to cope.

an artist can paint sun and light, and
he can hang it high,

but there are better hues, like blacks
and blues, that make the people cry.

the broken man in his darkest hour, can
stir the stagnant soul,

he shakes, and wakes, and once more
breaks, and what's deeper than a hole?

so when you cry, it is sublime, and you
become the art we seek,

your pain is real, we feel as you feel,
you're gorgeous when you're bleak.

Accessory.

you are my needle, you are my friend,
and there is nothing good in you.
you just enable, and pretend,
that i'm justified in what i do.
you say that self-destruction,
is natural, for it erases the weak,
you keep me too fucked up to function,
in a dysfunctional society.
sitting here in the darkness,
too high to know the sun has gone down,
this alley seems absolutely gorgeous,
i always wake up in a different part of
town.

you are my lover, you are my tool,
we use each other just to get off,
loving and leaving might sound cool,
but it has nothing to do with love.
you say that it's easier this way,
no relationship, just sex and go,
you keep me coming back to play,

what hurts me the most is what i don't know.

lying here ready to fuck and forget,

waiting for you in this filthy bed,

there's no protection, just ignorance,

how much of your disease has already spread?

you are my ending, you are my muse,

and i will use you to free me at last,

from a life of constant self-abuse,

and flashbacks to the abuse of the past.

you say that it's just that simple,

pull the trigger and let god sort out his mess,

you keep me still, as you press against my temple,

begging me to release and just say yes.

standing here frozen in time,

my life flashes before my eyes, and is done,

nothing in it worth saving, i realize,

i close my eyes, clench my fist, and i am gone.

Corruption.

he said i'd hate to corrupt you,

but i knew that he was lying.

besides, that's way too late to do,

but there's no harm in trying.

so when you bend my will,

and insert your own corruptions,

make sure the evil that you spill,

comes from more than your eruptions.

so plow the sweet earth below your feet,

and sow the seed you choose,

and when it grows, and you're ready to
eat,

it'll taste just dark enough for you.

he said, but honestly, i'd love to
corrupt you,

and soon after, he could no longer
speak.

i'm more corrupt than i appear, it's
true,

my seeds grow inside you, as you read
me.

i act so sweetly, you trust me
completely,

and i burn the earth where your garden
grows.

my evil is quiet, i cause riots neatly,

inside your heart, your head, your soul.

so while you think you're turning me,

ever so slowly, you're being turned.

you become just dark enough for me to
feed,

and plant my seed in the ground i
burned.

Carry Your God.

and he carried his god in his pocket,

day to day and age to age,

and in the end, was still destroyed by
life.

there was no remnant seen,

there was no apology from cosmic forces,

no sign of "well done,"

no juvenile tongues waving ceaselessly
like flags of feigned freedom,

his words, his ideals, his story.

and there was no talk of him,

save for the voice in the wind blowing
around the dust that he was.

and in what tongues and languages do
these blasphemies speak?

and what worlds are standing still,

awaiting the silent shatter of space-
time against their ethereal boundaries?

and when the blow comes hammering down

from the nonexistent dueling forces they
worship,

will the only tangible sign be another
sunrise?

another day radiating outward the will
of none but the universe:

that this planet should live,

that these people should fight,

that this man should be remembered.

but alas, for some, there is no blow,

no force awakening them once more,

no more sunrises boiled up and out by
fusion from the depths of space,

rocketing across taken-for-granted
skies,

reaching the eyes of a people that used
to call it god.

for all, this time, this day, this hour
comes,

and we in our self-deemed infinite
wisdom have called it death.

and whose voice calls out in gusts of
memory and sand across desert and plain?

is it the dust of generations forgotten,
the song of the abyss?

and shall this dust of man, remnant of
those who stepped across dimensions,

and physics and space-time itself, be
rolled into a ball?

shall it be hardened into rock and
passed around as a reminder,

an heirloom of eternity and her
children?

and shall the people who live, against
all odds,

take and carry and cherish their
reminder?

yes, and yes,

and yes, and yes,

and yes.

and in this way, he will not be
forgotten,

they will not pass away unnoticed,

there will be, there has been, there is
indeed, a SIGN.

and you shall carry your ancestors about
with you,

your heritage, your past, present, and
future.

and you shall both carry, and be, the
sign, and the remnant.

and when the son of he who is no more,
who disappeared slowly,

thinking he would not be remembered,

carries the ground bones and dust of his
father,

his people, himself, as a reminder and
assurance,

then he will carry his god in his
pocket,

day to day, and age to age.

there is no more, there was no more,
there shall be no more than this.

all else is a blinding flash before
naive eyes.

carry your people, your fathers, your
sons, your past, present, future,
yourself,

and you will carry your god with you.

and in turn, he will carry you, if it so
happens that he is, and is more than we
can ever carry, or know.

Fireworks.

there's a hostage situation upstairs,
and no one cares.

2nd floor, 5th door down,
the lights have gone out.

a gunshot rang out at nine,
as they lit up the sky.

out the window is a big parade,
independence day.

all the neighbors are outside on the
street,
except for pete.

people die one by one as we sing,
let freedom ring.

Demon.

i wrestle with my demon,
and sometimes, he wins.

he only ever fucks me,
if i give up while i'm pinned.

his black and fiery semen,
is the epitome of sin,

and it burns a hole inside of me,
until i try again.

Today Is A Day Of Frailty.

today is a day of frailty.

today is silenced razors running down
backbones,

digging trenches and then planting
kisses that explode

with pain and aftershock down your fault
line.

today is holding on to escape, the wire
of failure unseen,

connected to nothing, a stone drop into
the darkness,

singing about freedom until crushed by
gravity and guilt.

today is the boot heel we lick on our
knees, a master above us, upon us,
inside us,

implanting and infecting us with
hopelessness and raw futile power;

we are subservient to the life we choose
and the love we cannot.

today is the broken-necked swan, cradled
and swallowed by the sea,

lopsided and slipping into waters once
tread so easily and with such pride;

the waves once kicked to propel you, are now kicking back.

today is interruption, a disconnect between the cerebral and the senses,

something has gotten between yourself, and no feeling can be trusted;

best not to walk today.

today is subtlety and chaos breeding in the smoky living room,

making silent, swift-footed new children that will

build adamantine walls only to burn the cities within them to the ground;

somewhere, someday, exhaling will mean murder.

today is god stubbing his toe upon prayers strewn lazily about the heavens,

waiting for someone to answer, or play with them;

he curses and kicks them, and walks away.

today is a day of whiplash lust, people thrown together too fast,

too hard, too many, and swarming upon themselves

to escape loneliness and conscience,

producing drugged dumpster babies and
new diseases to name and to care for;

both nurseries are painted with blood.

today is a gunshot wound fingered until
it orgasms in pain,

phallic white fingers in condom gloves
digging deeper,

searching frantically and surgically for
the clitoris bullet.

today is time slowing to a crawl while
you're in the midst of a blender,

slowly turning blades just missed with
matrix-style bends and twists,

trying to stay alive underwater with no
air and no hope for escape;

the top is on and all you're trying to
do is avoid dying gruesomely

ten long seconds earlier than you will
anyway.

today is a series of unending nightmares
for a coma patient,

there is no waking up and life consists
of one horrible scenario after another,
forever,

desperately praying for death, but
without the ability to so much as move
your lips;

caught in hell with only one exit pass,

and everyone above you is denying you
the privilege.

today is a day of frailty.

Expel.

The gag reflex throws itself up, there is nothing left to expel.

All out in the open, secrets of a recluse, vomited upon walking souls and stardust.

Covered in my innards, men who just knew me became me, demonstrating my pain and private sufferings to walled-up masses who never so much as drool a secret.

My stomach is so empty as to be nonexistent, the page regurgitated and all there is left to read is wet ink.

There are no words, the raw elements have been expunged from out of the pretension of syntax.

No articulation or description, just ink and the smell of acid-dissolved paper.

My love poems are ruined, there is nothing sweet left, the fermentation process has been disrupted.

Only the source material remains. I feel sick, I must lie down, while they decipher my insides, and operate on my organs, touching every hidden bloody thing I ever housed.

The cage of the monster is being cleaned out, the beast is being studied under harsh light.

They have cut out his tongue and all he can do is scream.

He loves his cage, we love our entrapments, safeties, hiding places that define us.

Places that we complain about being trapped within, but cannot do without.

Exposure is cold and bright, ugly and embarrassing.

Someone must reach in and pull out this lovely tumor I've grown attached to, bend down and suck out this delicious poison that I thrive upon.

Withdrawal begins, I cannot breathe, I need the fix you have taken.

I have expelled it all, and fucked myself inside out.

Can you see an entry point, an exit wound?

What shot through me so long ago with such incredible speed, or has it lodged itself comfortably against a ventricle?

Stop the heart to save my life, no metaphor now, I do not mean emotion.

My heart beats raw ink, pulsing and pumping whole books worth of pain, patient rage, and imprints of lovers' shoes on their way out.

Read that and get the fuck back to me. I am done.

I need to be rehydrated and fed, my mouth is closing in on accepting help, biting stubbornly down before they can spoon-feed me white lies back to health.

The raw beast drowns in alcohol and pure truth, being killed and preserved and jarred up in front of me.

It's like watching yourself die, there was nothing in me he did not exhibit the best of while showing us his worst.

He was mine, MINE! And what have you done? Healed me?

I cannot cough anymore, the virus that kept me coughing kept me breathing.

What did you do? Killed it.

There are no words, you have destroyed the best real poet that ever fucking lived in order to save the cage from rusting.

You make no fucking sense!

I have thrown up every dark and red demon for your study, for your principles, for you to say you saved me, but who said I wanted exorcism?

My gut hurts, there is nothing left to digest with, there is no middle ground between beauty and shit now.

Why am I still hungry? The beast was eating me alive, and feeding me at the same time: eating my brokenness and shitting out greatness in words, defecating brilliance right into my inky bloodstream.

What the fuck have you done? I cannot even recognize the power of this pen now, or write about how the beast in the jar looks at me, like me, through me, as me.

Can't even put into words how I can see him from across the room in his jar, and yet still taste alcohol in my now tongueless mouth.

I miss being eaten. The pain has nowhere to go but down and out, and nothing can ever turn it into beauty again.

You have coldly exhumed my soul, you have cleaned me, you have saved me, and you know what?

I FUCKING HATE YOU FOR IT!!!

The raw bloody lump of brilliance on the floor could have been a masterpiece, but I guess you wanna study the bird embryo inside of the broken egg, and kill it in the process, instead of learning things from watching it grow up and fly.

The only way you learn is to dissect, exorcise, kill, exhume, preserve, and expel!

And you still haven't learned a goddamn thing!!!

Rites.

the name has been lost to us,

we do not remember the incantation,

the rhythm stays and sways throughout
history,

and becomes the backdrop for sacrifices
called by another name.

i have no idea if the words ever
existed,

but the voices that sang did, and are no
more.

the urging trapped between spirit and
throat has been exorcised from out of
foreign mouths,

and burst forth as a million more urges
and stories passed down by drunken
divinity.

there is a god in my tongue.

the trees remember the whispers that
bent them closer to us,

the soil still carries the dried blood
spilled as passion became price,

and the word became flesh.

the ritual carved in stone has been
replaced with fire-branded commandments,

and the goddess of an ancient tribe took
4,000 years to grow a penis and morph
into the god of the covenant.

evil became ensnared with good, and both
were thrown away and replaced by the
current hybrid,

in the guise of a dichotomy.

the name has been lost to us,

and the flesh of mortal fathers became
the blood of god's son.

no sacrifice brings rain, and no spell
awakens the moon.

blood for my god is the same blood for
their gods,

the high priestess becomes evangelist,

the sooth-sayer becomes the prophet,

and the spellbook becomes the hymnal.

The Beauty of the Fall.

> *"like the song of the wind in a*
> *burning building,*
>
> *a long look holding the whole world*
> *suspended,"*
>
> *--- Octavio Paz. From "Sun Stone."*

the beauty of the fall is such

that time can stop and hold so much,

within a moment of fading, crystallized,

the sweet swan song of sating, realized.

the end is framed, the world stops
spinning,

and the end looks much like the
beginning.

chaotic, swirling, forming fresh worlds

from the supernova of a death, unfurls,

a new creation out of ashes still
smoldering,

the beauty of the fall is never knowing,

what beautiful new thing is now forming.

the moment held between pillars of time,

and obituary lines, is seen as art, a
design,

the variables shifted into place,

the outcome coming as outer space,

makes room for embryonic days,

by birthing them in the ones that fade.

the aftermath becomes a miracle anew,

and as it is born, we mourn the death
too,

indeed, the greatest memorial to the
fallen,

is the rising of the new to its calling.

memory is remembered in the action,

destiny is honored in the connection.

time is framed, the whole world hushed,

and then life resumes speeding past,
rushed.

the beauty of the fall, is the rose in
the hand

of the falling man, as it plummets with
him,

and imparts seeds to the ground as it
crashes,

and in the wreckage of ending, becoming
ashes,

but each seed has the chance to grow a
new rose,

and so the cycle continues as the world
grows.

this is the birth and death sequence of
all,

so i must marvel at the genius,

at the beauty of the fall.

Heavy.

she said she slid a blade across her arm
last night, and i sighed.

"wow really? damn, that's some heavy
shit," i say.

i'm leaning against a shabby looking
railing,

looking up at the gray sky and fiddling
with some pocket object, and my phone.

someone please call me, and get me out
of this,

give me a reason to defer, distract, to
say i have to go.

but my battery is low, so forget it.

i don't think i can take her telling me
this.

i think i'm angry, but i don't act like
i care.

she follows me outside, and leans with
her arms hanging off the side,

cigarette precariously perched between
her fingers some three stories above
certain death.

she tells me her ex-boyfriend came over
a week ago

to smoke pot and fuck, and wound up
stealing her meds.

"is that right? that sunofabitch."

i don't really give two shits about him,

but i figure it's all background noise
anyway.

what else can i say?

this chick is a mindfuck, i'm telling
you,

but i like her, i guess.

i didn't really start listening to her
talk until the part about cutting.

my scarred wrists have ears.

i pull my sleeves down a little tighter
around them,

as if i wanted to deafen them from what
else she might say.

and as if on cue, she returns to the
subject,

"so anyway, he's part of the reason why
i cut last night.

i'm just so damn frustrated with him,
and there's no other outlet, you know?"

'heh, you could try writing,' i thought
to myself.

"well, you shouldn't do that anymore,

i don't want to get any calls about you,
no one is worth you doin that."

i am such a fucking hypocrite.

i sound concerned because,

well i guess i am.

i mean don't get me wrong,

the only reason i know this chick is
business as usual.

we do our thing, and go our separate
ways.

but i figure, even fuck buddies have a
code or something, right?

well, i do, anyway.

she shifts on the rail, and looks at me
all serious.

this is going to sting, i know her.

"yeah well, that's all well and good,

but let's be blunt here,

you wouldn't even be here today if you
weren't fucking me.

i mean, if you really care, well, i
guess you could,

you're not like anthony or anything,

but i guess i just need a way out,

and i'm not trying to make you it or whatever,

but, dammit i need something.

hey, can you maybe give me a ride somewhere?"

i don't know why, but the first thought in my mind was "junkie,"

but in the hopes that i was wrong,

(and also because, duh, i fucked her today,

you'd think i'd notice track marks on her arm,

instead of razor lines of dried blood,)

i decided to say, "yeah sure, where you need to go?"

it goes without saying that with my salary,

and in this economy, i drive a piece of shit honda.

actually, that's a lie, i drive my mother's piece of shit honda,

and god help me should i ding or dent or scratch

her already twice banged up, puke yellow piece of shit honda.

"to the grocery store. i get about $200 in food stamps,

and it's about time to restock the snackage pantry,

get some more booze, cigarettes, and a few box meals."

"sure, we can stop at Super Saver Plus. my uncle used to be a stocker there."

if she heads for the aisle with razors in it,

i'll hope she just needs to shave, but i'll still be nervous.

'if only i was here last night,' i tell myself,

'maybe i could have proved i cared, and stopped her from being an idiot.'

yeah, because my experiences have rendered me as wise,

and not full of shit or backsliding at all.

but that's beside the point.

we both throw our jackets on, lock the door,

and walk down three quick flights of stairs.

i unlock my mommies' disgusting precious p.o.s.

and we just sit there for a while after i crank it up,

with our hands to the heater, waiting for it to kick in.

i steal a quick glance at her.

something grabs me inside, out of nowhere, and strong.

i honestly don't know if it was pity, love,

or some sickening new emotion in between,

but i threw myself upon her, lips touching lips,

and my hands finding their way to her already warm sides.

what was this? i wasn't horny, and she isn't even really my type.

we made out for a good 5 minutes, which surprised me,

because i expected her to immediately back off and be like, "what the fuck?"

when we broke lips, and my fingers uncurled themselves from around her hips,

i looked at her with a fiery passion
usually alien to me

unless i'm pissed, drunk, horny, or all
three.

"if you ever cut yourself again, i will
fucking leave,

and you won't see me again, ever. i just
can't, i can't take it."

so there it was, heavy and hanging in
the tense silence

somewhere between romance and reality,

between anger and compassion.

there was nothing that could be done
about it.

it was like, yeah, this just happened.

she started to say something, but it
became indistinguishable

as words became sudden sobs,

which heaved her tiny body like a ship
on the angry sea.

i held her as she cried, and The Eagles
came on the oldies station.

i turned up "take it easy," as i let my
arms enfold her.

i guess i cared a lot more than i
thought i did.

no wonder the sex was so good.

i mean, we both know what it's like to
cut.

i think...

i think i love her.

whew.

now that's heavy.

Oh Fragile Heart, Fuck Off!

oh fragile heart,
fuck off!
i need you to be strong,
stop breaking anew with each beat,
toughen up, grow some balls.
this isn't love,
this is kind defeat,
and i tire of taking the fall.
thorn after thorn,
on a headless rose,
you rise each morn,
stabbing yourself in hopes
of reaching some pinnacle,
and the ghost
is identical
to what the real thing would be,
if it ever existed,
i can almost see the petals,
smelling sweetly, lightly misted!
fucking idiot, quit climbing
the ladder to going down,

and let your wounds heal

before wearing another crown

of thorns like her,

like him,

like them all,

this hurt

is prelude to a fall.

oh fragile heart,

fuck off!

i need you to get mean,

stab the heartbreakers with the shards,

and revel in the screams,

cause it's her turn to cry,

and it's his turn to cry,

so take the shrapnel they made,

and make them ask themselves why,

they like to break beautiful things

just for the fun of it,

listen my darling,

i've had my run of it!

so this time be a bitch,

bite back, and draw blood,

scratch the foolish love itch,

until you're sated, then run

like hell!

and oh well if you're a romantic, suck
it in,

get yours, close the door,

and save the heartbreak for them.

oh fragile heart,

fuck off!

no more silent,

no more soft,

be violent,

like ice,

look good,

look nice,

slip and break

all the ones

who would walk on you,

and be done,

be unforgiving,

just for fun.

harden up,

grow a thick skin,

let them earn love,

or being let in,

there is no sin,

in destroying them,

(all the women,

and all the men,)

in literature.

flay the skin

of those who neglected you,

disrespected you,

and infected you with promises

they defected from,

don't be dumb,

the gullible are drunk on love,

being fattened up,

on the romantic drug,

just so she or he can shove em,

into the oven,

to be roasted and toasted,

while the cook is boasting.

fuck that, i'll look nice,

and destroy you with a look,

bitch, it's my time to shine,

and your time to cook!

so cook on, my dear,

i got my deep fryer near,

because i got your fucking recipe right
here!

oh fragile heart,

fuck off!

fuck them,

and get lost.

i hate to be crude,

and i've never been rude,

i've stuck around and held you,

and written poetry too,

but the favor so earned,

was never returned,

and though i kept you warm,

it was MY ass that was burned,

so i've learned to let go,

and let god sort out the mess,

and in the end, i know,

that whether pants or a dress,

i guess i'll be hurt

well, that is, unless,

i protect myself,

from their cruel ugliness.
i'm tired of this game,
and i've had quite enough,
and so i thus proclaim:
oh fragile heart,
fuck off!

Resolve.

I fucking hate this part.

Where is a goddamn sing-song montage
when you need one?

Where is the quick fix, the star-wipe
solution,

the miracle that swings in and saves the
day?

Why must I always want the easy part,
and put up with the hard?

Don't I deserve a break today?

Somebody just shit all over my dream,
after all the work I've done,

and I'm supposed to let that go?

Sometimes there IS no moving on, there's
just moving through.

I cannot stand that I have to change
plans once again,

and settle for less until I actually
deserve more.

This is the grind, this is paying your
dues,

this is sludging through the shit to get
to what?

The remnants of a dream?

A fragmented slice of hope?

It's not worth it.

And to get to the things in this life that are,

you have to deal with more shit.

I really fucking hate this part.

It's like my life has been stuck on the sad downtime, crying hero part of the movie for years.

You know?

The part right before they sing a song while fixing things,

or call in friends and team up on it,

or figure something crucial out, beat the bad guys and get the girl?

Where is all of that?

And what if you're also a bad guy?

Does that make me an antihero?

I don't know, but the game is getting old,

and the movie is stuck on a loop.

I just want the next chapter to start before I do something crazy, like tear the page, or god forbid, burn the book.

I've shown what strength I have left in this situation.

But I'm wearing thin, and trying to stick to all these scary new plans

I've written up, faking optimism and courage.

God, please supersize what resolve is left in me.

You told me if I showed the effort, you would back me up.

You told me to be patient.

You also told me that while you don't like ALL of my poems,

they have a right to be written, heard, and read.

Anyway, you have given me amazing friends whom I would not be here without.

And though sketchy at times, my health could be a lot worse.

And you gave me this gift, which I am using now.

So help me get to the next level,

ascend to the next stage of enlightenment,

and beat the crap out of my demons.

Maybe I should start singing Bon Jovi,

drink a Red Bull and just work on what I can, a little at a time.

Cause it's never ever like the movie,

but I can make this mine, and I can be the hero.

Give me more resolve to climb these mountains, and more patience.

It won't be easy, but as long as we stick together,

maybe there really "ain't no mountain high enough."

And as corny as that was, so are montages, and star-wipes,

and dramatic cheesy endings where the guy wins and gets the girl,

but in a completely unrealistic way.

And maybe I don't need any of those.

But I will take that win,

because by then,

I'll have earned it.

letter to god from a man on a tiny speck
in time and space somewhere in your
universe

dear god,

down here, instead of remaining quiet
and listening for you and trusting
instinct and meditating on what would
really work by using our minds and
working together, we've come up with
this funny little thing called religion.
we sing songs, we preach and are
preached at, we find and decode and
study old books that we base our lives
and families around. we start wars over
others who do the same in a different
way, worshiping either what they
perceive as the same god, or an entirely
different one altogether. we kill each
other screaming the names we make up for
you, and we kill ourselves in your
honor, or because it's all your fault.
we build christian communities where we
live, and destroy whole cities over
there in that heathen land, with its
heathen god, and now i cannot tell the
difference between who is who. we swear
oaths by you, we fear your wrath, we put
your name on our currency, and our
buildings. we pick the parts of the book

we like, and abhor the rest, and every
other book claiming to have been written
by you. we stress late at night and
wrack our brains with ways to keep what
we call sin at bay. what sins are sins
and what sins are worse is always
debatable and everyone has an opinion
and everyone has a bias and we worry
ourselves to death over how we're viewed
in our communities and churches based on
the law of god, as we call it, and
what's right and proper. we make up a
story and we make up two alternate
endings which supposedly we will end up
in after death based on how we live. the
good place we call heaven, the bad one
is hell, and because every brainwashing
has to have an other, we make up a devil
and blame all bad things that happen in
our lives, which in nature is just
called life, survival of the fittest, on
him, and we tell each other that we must
be saved from ourselves and the devil by
your son, jesus, using pieces of
mythology that existed long before he
was supposed to exist, and we create a
wonderful story. it really is something
else. i don't know really what to make
of it all, but i bought into it before,
got out of it, came back, and now i'm a
part of a wonderful church that has

great people in it, and finally is one
that accepts me for me, when all others
have failed using illogical criteria to
outcast us such as sexuality, and that's
another letter, but i just want you to
know that if i'm wrong and all this is
true, i'm sorry and i hope you
understand, but i really doubt you're
gonna throw me away for my nature after
everything you and i, i'd like to
believe, have been through. it's been an
incredible, painful, mind-blowing,
enlightening trip, and i don't think
it's as simple as heaven and hell,
although we make our own down here, and
i think you have more foresight and
sense than they think you do, and i just
want to be sure i'm doing the right
thing here, not because i'm afraid of
heaven or hell anymore, or even the
people that at times can get nutty about
you, but because i want to be remembered
as a good man who did good things and
accepted everyone, even though most
people will not surprise you when it
comes to disappointing or hurting you.
if all of this is real, and i'm doomed,
then i've wasted very little time
thinking and worrying about it on the
grand scale, and in that case, i guess i
better do a lot more living before i

burn forever. and if i'm right and it's all way more wonderful and mysterious than anyone could ever guess, and that it's more about transcendence and oneness than wrong and right, angels and demons, then we all have so much more to look forward to. either way, i just want a little tiny push in the right direction. i'm waiting quietly with my arms open as i hope my mind is, and i'm listening, god. you don't have to write back. just reward me for having the sense to be still and listen, by assurance in its smallest form, by just a little push in the direction you'd have me go. i'm about to marry a christian and join a church and i just need to know what you'd have me do. i'm not dumb enough to ask why, or to guess. i'm listening, and i know you can hear me. thanks for everything.

your poet in residence,

bear.

I Am In Love With The Mystery Of Dark Stars...

i am in love with the mystery of dark
stars,

of dingy hotel bathrooms,

of submissive men orbiting fat ugly
women like sad moons,

of sudden spasms of greatness in the
night,

of cigar smoke,

of dead things that haven't been buried,
like the bill of rights,

of unseen planes and their window-
worshipping tenants,

of men who populate parks when the sun
goes down,

of the inner workings of the heart of a
dominatrix,

of the link between music and
transcendence,

of faithless healers,

of jazz without sound,

of the wind wrapping leaves around an
invisible figure,

of jaded women's contempt,

of the beauty in tearing something
apart,

of breathing with words,

of one hand clapping morse codes to god,

of the speed of pain versus the instant
of pleasure,

of female orgasms in all their
thunderous glory,

of the angels that spoke to mozart,

of the demons that haunted bukowski,

of death's hungry mouth, a gaping hole
in the earth,

of joy in the bottomless pit,

of lovers wrestling in bed, naked and
flailing,

of the instantaneous feel of an eight-
minute long ray of sun,

of the melodies of empty bottles and
emptier men,

of tightrope hopes above hell,

of life before life after death,

of this moment which passed just seconds
ago, but can never be reached again,

of people's judgments of people,

of the tiny specks of dust hanging in
the air and in space, dirt all the same,

of the grandeur of dragonflies,

of nothing really being unknown, and in
that way, erasing all mysteries at once,

and unifying everything as nothing,
which is unknown.

Bonfires Of Contention.

snow.

ash trees falling.

footsteps into dark.

bonfires of contention.

winter with my father.

snapshot of hidden contempt.

revelations.

snow.

I Want Something Real.

i want something real,

i want to hold it in my hand, fluttering
and defiant of capture.

i don't want something shiny, something
pleasing, or something popular.

i want something that bleeds.

i want something that bites.

i want something that knows when to flee
and how to fight,

something that will take you on over the
things that it loves.

i want something real.

i don't want eye-candy,

i don't want perfect script on expensive
paper,

over-analyzed by nearly dead men who
know nothing of the true currents that
flow underneath.

i want vengeance harnessed and furious,
ready to tear someone asunder at a
moment's notice.

i want an arsenal of soul-ripping truth
dispensed freely by words who just got
out of rehab,

got their car repoed, and have a bitch
for an ex-wife.

i want something real.

i don't want a particularly selected
strand of words guaranteed to make your
audience cry,

i don't want clichés and obvious wisdoms
bottled into a bundle of rhymes,

and tossed like a grenade at readers too
drunk or stupid to notice.

i don't want an emo's angry ink-smeared
and tear-stained poem about why life
sucks,

and nietzsche is the closest thing he'll
have to a father.

i want words that have no agenda, no
bias, no allegiance to their master,

words that defy because they can, and
offend because you're a pussy,

words that tell you off with the fury of
bukowski, the diction of wilde,

the bravery of whitman, and the godlike
voice of paz!

i want something real.

something with emotion, without getting
emotional,

something idealistic, but not always optimistic,

something perseverant, but never static,

something alive, yet immortal.

i want something with teeth,

that feels pain but converts it to a power that others have never known,

that sees the horrors of the world, as well as the beauty it contains,

that breathes, alive, fearful, and imperfect on the page, (take me as i am,)

something as wondrous and rare,

as vile and broken,

as tough and as fragile,

as fallible and gritty,

as creative and thoughtful,

as naked and free,

as fleshy and proud,

as happy and loud,

as pleasing to the crowd,

as me.

i want it to be just like me,

and in a way, just like you.

i want something real,
and only that will do,
because then, and only then,
am i writing my truth.

Reproach Of The Muse.

once again, i invoked the muse,

well, that was a mistake,

she brought cheap booze and razorblades.

i want a poem without the pain.

she says, "there's no growth without rain."

fuck that! i don't need torture to produce a masterpiece.

bitch, please!

all of my lines dripping in blood, is not fine.

"but if it's not your blood, then they're not your lines."

shut the fuck up, i'll just go on writer's block for a while then.

"that's for you to heal up, before you're ripped apart again."

i know, and IT FUCKING SUCKS! it's so not worth this shit.

none of it.

"so i guess i can erase this world-changing masterpiece, and be done with it?"

would the pain be worth it?

"i can't tell you that, but it's a lot."

who will it change?

"i can't tell you that, but it's a lot."

how long is it?

"i can't tell you that, but it's a lot."

how long will it be known?

"i can't tell you that, but it's a lot."

what can you tell me?

these scars still aren't healing, but
i'm proud,

cause i got something in return,

what will i get for this one now?

"i can't tell you that..."

but it's A LOT???

bullshit, you said all that before.

"you have no idea, do you?"

no, and while i'm alive, i never will.

"and when you're dead, you can't write
anymore, or feel.

so get to it while you can. they love
you, man! "

no, they love YOU, i'm just a tool of
pain and syntax.

metaphor and malevolence, rhyme and
weakness.

"but without his tools, what can a
builder do?"

he's god! so, DUH, anything he fucking
wants to!

"but more glory is made by greatness
pouring from the bruised,

the broken, the underdog, the humble
meek."

and whose glory? his, and i hate to say
it, but what about me?

keep your booze and bruises, razors and
abuses,

dying bones, be gone, because i fucking
refuse this.

i'm done, go torture somebody else.

your masters' heaven is riding on the
backs of those in hell.

the devil is his tool, he doesn't need
me,

so take it all, i quit, take my poetry.

give me my life, the one i earned, let
me start anew,

i may need god, but writing hurts, so i
don't need you.

i rebuke the muse, and stomp upon the
phoenix ashes,

i resign, i'm through, and you can kiss
all of our asses,

all of the poets, who are tired of this
game you play,

"but you don't know that! at least
they're brave enough to stay,

and stick it out for the pay, the
published books, the adoring fans,

but you don't care, you could have been
the greatest man to have ever written
poetry, despite the things that he's
been through, since whitman, kid!

but now that dream doesn't go to you.

selfish little shit, impatient like so
many other writers,

this poem could've been it, an anthem
for all of the survivors.

but you gave all that up, and you speak
for those way more mature,

you really don't give a fuck about
poetry, you just wanna be adored.

tired of the pain? tough shit. and if
you don't need my help,

guess i'll leave then, james. what a
waste of talent, go fuck yourself!!!"

To Remember.

he walked across the street,

and he was already pissed when he got up
that morning.

the voices in his head were having a
conference,

and none of them liked each other.

it felt like the sun was shining behind
his eyes,

and he was sure that they were back
there flicking switches.

he threw the sheets off angrily,

and wondered if the goddamn sun would
sleep in just once.

he dressed himself and flung the door
open,

heading for the nearest liquor store.

"breakfast of fucking champions," he
thought to himself,

as he slapped his money down and grabbed
his bottle-in-a-bag.

he stood in the sun, he could've been
anyone standing there,

but he wasn't anything.

just a dinosaur who lived on alcohol and easy pussy.

he wasn't sorry ever for anything, for this was how the play had been written,

the backstory made sense, and the lines were loud and mad,

hell, the script was unfinished, but he was gonna play it a scene at a time,

audience or none.

he brushed by a woman, and looked back with disgust.

"i hate people," he said, and crossed the street back to his apartment.

up in his room, he smoked a cigar and ripped the bottle out of the brown paper bag.

he opened it, and began drinking.

he was still brewing with rage, and it made him angrier not knowing why.

he banged out a poem on his remington portable typewriter.

it read:

"i seek solace from myself, a peace i cannot find,

if genius is madness and war is hell, i'll surely lose my mind.

my heart was sold for silence, and my
body traded for booze,

the rest boils with inner violence, now
my mind i fear i'll lose."

he backed away from the typewriter, and
looked slowly at his words.

in an amnesiac moment, he grabbed for
the telephone, and dialed marie's
number.

some stranger with a foreign accent
answered him.

he hung it up.

another little light went on in his
mind,

and a voice said, "oh yeah, that's why
i'm pissed.

she's gone, and no one else will ever
listen to me the way she did."

a tear raced down the lines of his
weathered face, and he sighed,

and said to himself, "and that's why i
drink. to forget."

he sat back down, and looked at his
typewriter.

the voice, in a whisper, returned.

"and that's why you write. to remember."

The Word Became Flesh, And The Word Was Pain.

the word became flesh, and the word was pain.

and that's me.

headphones, zeppelin, observing.

crowds look like talons and beaks,

clamoring for another messiah,

another new thing to dispose of.

hot rain and air conditioning don't mix,

my goose bumps are vomiting.

i feel the metamorphoses killing me.

cocoon is tomb.

i feel connected to disillusion.

it seems right that everything is wrong.

i just want enough books to waste me away.

replace the dust, read until i'm on a page, or am one.

sunday evening never felt so dismal.

the guillotine of guilt awaits,

and i must free myself from the shackles.

i cannot look in your eyes anymore
without feeling like somehow,

i'm slowly destroying everything you
stand for.

but i love you for who you are.

i am a madhouse buzzing beneath the
pristine innocence of my words.

i am a murderer donning the face of a
child.

i love the way i look when i'm truly
happy.

has nothing to do with how i look.

i don't hate my smile so much when you
make me laugh.

only the idea of laughing without you.

greatness is creativity plus repetition,
i've always thought.

no one gave a damn about campbell's
tomato soup cans until warhol.

On a different note, i never knew a bank
could fuck you so hard.

one slip up, and there they go, charging
you for breathing wrong.

no groceries this week, but we'll live.

my chest, my side, my back, hell, my whole body seems to be strategically trying to destroy master control.

the spirit is willing, but the flesh is traitorous.

fuck you, too.

i used to think pain was an annoying monkey wrench in the engine,

but lately god is showing me that pain is more like gasoline:

it can burn you until you die, or you can FUCKING USE THAT SHIT to go anywhere.

not like writing is getting me out of this dump. it never got me out of the others.

never stopped me from being poor and almost homeless,

or stopped me from being a regular at every local hospital since i was born,

or stopped one of mom's boyfriends beating on her in front of me.

he just keeps swinging, everything does, swinging right at us,

and the pen can do nothing for anyone.

that pen though, it is the thing that helps me convert pain to promise.

it uses the gasoline of pain to produce glory, drop by drop.

it helps me survive even when i don't want to.

you know, it sure would be fucking easier,

dying a victim to something i was born with.

but here i am, writing again, alive,

feeling every miserable thing god ever intended to use on me

to get me to realize that i'm above it all.

not below.

that i can use it.

and the writing doesn't have to be brilliant to change lives.

but it helps.

the word became flesh, and the word was pain.

and that's me.

Fires Unseen.

i still make promises i don't keep,

i still fall down and blame my knees,

i still lie and justify it,

i still cry because of trees,

i guess i'll learn,

there are fires unseen,

but i still burn.

i still protest getting out of bed,

i still make monsters with my head,

i still write, but i'm full of shit,

i still say poetry's better when i'm
dead,

the world will turn,

there are fires unseen,

and we all burn.

i still commit little suicides,

i still believe everything is finite,

i still remember roses in the pit,

i still believe the great ones never
die,

or so i yearn,

there are fires unseen,

so enjoy the burn.

i still pray to gods long extinct,

i still know pain, but it makes me
think,

i still believe girls play hard to get,

i still wonder just how all of this is
linked,

it makes me churn,

there are fires unseen,

love is to burn.

"Hey, Kid"

*"my poems are only bits of scratchings
on the floor of a cage."*

--- *Charles Bukowski.*

He told me to latch on to something
real, to dig deep,

and pull that demon out, and say,
"Alright motherfucker, let's talk! "

He told me to ignore the women, unless
horny,

(had no earthly idea I also favored men,
and I kept it that way,)

to drink when necessary, to write when
it's fresh,

and to go toe-to-toe with every disease
or demon the fucking gods could conjure
up.

Fuck 'em.

To be a badass, even though I was so
thin,

to be a bony little sack of fuck you and
eat shit.

To leave a candle in my darknesses so
the monsters inside me could see me,

and know the face of the son-of-a-bitch
who whipped their ass.

"That little pissant fucker could
fight!"

To get laid when I could, and to
eviscerate the bitch in writing if I
couldn't.

"Hell, do it anyway, grudge fucks are
fun," he said.

To know just how important the little
things were,

and just how dark it can be here, even
in the daylight.

"Shadows can't exist without the sun,"
he said.

"Good line, you should write tha---
Fuck, nevermind that, sorry," I said
back.

He just grinned.

To be glad if you didn't exist to
certain people,

and to be wary of praise of any kind.

He whispered roughly, "If they really
like your shit,

they'll be too busy writing and crying
to tell you you're a genius."

To respect silence, and the coming day that death would win,

and to just enjoy it, because who needs this shit?

To steer clear of religion and god, but know that the real prayer comes in desperation,

from lips that have tasted blood, and hands that know what it is to be broken.

To be happy that I was a "poor, word-hungry, book-loving little shit," as he put it,

because that's a passion money can't touch, and time can't dissolve.

Then he stood up, exhaling smoke, and told me, "Now, it's time you fucked off, kid."

I replied, "Fuck you, asshole, it's my dream! "

We nodded our respects to each other,

and he disappeared, smiling through a cigar.

If You Knew Him, You'd Understand.

I leaned over and asked the lady at the counter for a pen and paper.

She tossed 'em my way, and I thanked her, thinking of her fat round ass.

I sat down and began to write:

"I have 1979 in my pocket, and I don't ever care to specify whether it's money, (everyone's guess,) or the date.

One more penny and disco is dead."

A table down, some geeks were discussing the fact that everyone is made of stardust, to some older guy.

He scoffed and shouted, "Fuck the goddamn stars, I wanna be made of money! "

And I thought, "You stupid fuck, I wish you were too so I could burn you and legally get away with it. You're dust either way."

Some fat kid puked on me yesterday at a birthday party. He was in the middle of apologizing profusely when I stopped him. Sloughing regurgitated beenie-weenies and God knows what else from my clothes, I said,

"That's ok, you porky little shit, I needed a new suit anyway, and you could stand to lose the weight. Enjoy the party, pudgy."

I giggled about it a little, and kept writing:

"Our country shits on me. Reek, stench of liberty. Off me, it flings. Land where my father died, Land of pilgrim's genocide, and as the natives cried, they set evil free! "

Then I spaced a bit on the page, and wrote:

"I'm Roman because I like to watch. I'm Greek because I like the cock. I'm British because I'm a classy lay. I'm Iranian because I'll blow you away. I'm German because I'm a solid "Nein! " I'm American because I'm young and fine. I'm French because I'll love you passionately. Doesn't matter where, I'll screw you internationally! "

I laughed to myself and looked up.

The geeks were gone, and the old man was furiously doing a crossword puzzle.

I shook my head and looked behind me at the rows of poetry books.

I spaced again and wrote:

"I follow the rules that tell me to rhyme, I follow them with rhythm some of the time. Other times I say 'Fuck rhyme and rhythm, and fuck the rules of repetition, fuck the rules of repetition!' What's that you say? I'm rhyming still? Well it's my fucking poem, if I want to, I will! And maybe I'll use free verse and brevity too, and in that case, asshole, fuck you!"

I sighed and stretched, hating the song playing overhead.

I blocked it out and switched gears: "My soul is so big, it encompasses the entire, ever-expanding goddamn universe. And I am so small, I don't even fucking exist. And somewhere between the two, against all odds, these words appear: microorganisms, planets, leaves, the wind, love. I am nothing holding everything, writing something that could be anything, but it's not. It's just a thing that happened. Somewhere between the two, I represent what the world calls God. Either everywhere and everything, or nonexistent. But no matter which, he wrote a poem. It just happened. We just happened."

I paused and stood up.

I walked to get a refill.

Two girls were reading from one book, and making notes in it, IN PEN.

I winced and shook my head.

I sat back down with my drink and thought about my funny little quirks,

like loving books so much, that it bothers me to see someone even remotely damage them.

My eyes were tired, and the bookstore would be closing soon.

"One more," I whispered to myself.

One more:

"He was the kind of guy that pulls the tongues on his shoes a bit too high, and who liked velcro. He wears socks on his feet at almost all times, even when sleeping naked, because his feet get cold, and also because he hates his feet. His favorite blue jeans have a hole in them on one leg, and a diamond drawn in ink on the other. Today, his shirt is black, with metal studs, and one too many breast pockets. It makes him feel like an anguished rock star. His lucky hat is green with an off-center argyle stripe, a paperboy hat, and he wears it way too much. His stance is a proud limp, and his face is contemplative. An old soul in a young man's body, with an even younger man's face, and an even older man's bones. A living paradox. He is complicated, sensitive, grim, silly, uncensored, witty, deep, proud, loving, brave, naive, and made amazingly whole in his brokennesses. If you knew him, you'd understand."

For Charles Bukowski, and for my pallbearers.

(It will make them smile.)

Dancing In The Storm.

I dance in the storm,
the rain is falling thick,
and everybody warns
that I will get sick.

But I'm already there,
lightning masks my face
in its darkest stare,
and I dance anyway.

So I choose to dance,
even though I fear
the very circumstance
that brought me here.

And I choose to run,
with the wind and rain,
the lightning is my sun,
thunder is my name.

Thunder is my name.

Plea.

when i go to bed angry,
and i can't stand to let you see me,
don't let me fall asleep.

when i turn away,
too afraid of what i might say,
hold my hand, and be quiet with me.

don't let me accidentally
let you go, because i know i would fade.

don't let little things come between us,
because they aren't so little anyway.

when i forget why you love me,
and my heart is full of doubt,
if you have to, squeeze it out.

when i tell little white lies,
and disguise my intentions,
kiss me til truth is all i can mention.

if i give up, just show me love,
and i promise you, i'll try again.

if i fall down, just pick me up,
or fall with me until we both land.

The Christian.

and lo, i walked thru the kingdom of
bent knees and shattered souls,

and mocked "delusional" crosses of
silver and gold,

and though i loved god, the rest of this
show was shunned,

and i wrote that i doubted the existence
of his son,

and the bells rung, the songs sung, but
my ears were plugged,

and i called the book falsehood, and i
laughed like a thug,

and i ran far from steeples, though they
littered the miles,

and i feared any people with folded
hands and wide smiles,

and i swore i still loved god, but
doubted the rest,

and the rest hated my kind, and voted
themselves best,

and in my hiding place, i ignored all
the rituals, signs,

and i called them mislead, and
misleading, and unkind,

and i closed myself off in the secular world,

and i read books and heard songs with no christian words.

but one day god sent me his own, who loved me god's way,

he was what i once disowned, but i couldn't look away,

he was a good man, a kind man, the best man i'd seen,

and he gently held my hand, and told me he loved me,

and i loved him anyway, crosses or none at all,

and he didn't try to change me, for he loved all my soul,

and i began to understand that with no other evidence,

that christ lived, that i trusted, i saw christ live in him.

he doesn't use his faith for platforms of hate or of greed,

he just loves me completely, gives me all that i need,

and i know that god sent him to restore my faith,

and though i still am no christian, if
he were any other way,

i wouldn't love him as much, for he
showed me god's love,

and i love him as such that when i look
at him, or above,

i know that whatever the truth is about
god and the lost,

i will cling to the man who clings to
his cross.

For Randy, who is my rock.

El Poeta Sangra.

(The Poet Bleeds.)

1.

In this hour, passing slowly, like the
beating wings of moths drunk on light,
time steps with ashen feet.

Life and Death within each movement;
pray it does not turn its head.

I lie paralyzed by the arms of fate, and
the absence of my lover.

Night seeds blow around outside, finding
fertile ground in a moonlight garden
veranda.

Blood spills, runs, gushes, somewhere in
the city; a city not of broken dreams,
but one in which all the dreamers are
dead.

No dreams, only sleep, only death.

Only blood in the mass of confusion
known as the city.

The city loves hours, and eats them
hungrily.

But time hates a place, knows only a
destination, walking there quickly,
slowly, with ever-steady metronome feet.

2.

Each and every one of my nerves are tiny
souls that dance whenever I touch any
part of you.

They weep whenever they touch anything
else.

Thus, your absence is my pain.

Nothing else compares to touching you.

My body acts like you are a part of it.

Symbiotic legs cross,

magnetic arms grasp,

there has never been such a oneness in
all the history of love or numbers.

Skin rubs skin like the sea upon white
sands.

Caressing, lapping, ever-returning with
new gifts.

I hope the sea never dries up.

Half the world would die with it.

I would already be dead by the time the last drop of water evaporated.

Tongues explore familiar lands with the same curiosity and excitement as the first time they met.

Hands are buried like treasures, within each other, guarding other treasured things.

The city spins and throws the weak aside, a merry-go-round of the desolate and determined.

No hellish rides tonight, only love games and pleasure rides.

You are not a player, or a prize.

You are the game, and I know all the secrets, all the twists and turns.

I hold the book of lover's cheat codes.

Others want to play you, but I play to win.

The game is won.

We are one.

One is well.

3.

One explodes.

I turn and rise in my bed.

A bad dream, a worse reality.

Living nightmare, indeed.

The sun sits waking, on a horizon heavy
with smog and dark days ahead.

I turn to find you, I rise to find
myself,

I stand to become one.

Sunlight shows the face of God in a
woman.

I close the blinds, wishing only to see
the face of a woman.

God stands outside my window, blocked by
love and ambition.

The nape of your neck is tempting, but
only my dreams should end violently this
morning.

Your hand seems alone, yet I refrain.

I kiss you softly and return to
oblivion.

It is still early, I rejoin you in nothingness, in everything collapsed within a single breath.

Ours, synchronized, overlapping, steady, a Zen prayer.

Everything lies in nothing, as time blazes by, lit by its own fires, burned by the finger of God.

He wants my time, He gets only my oblivion-laced praises.

Songs in the night I do not know I sing.

Yet still, most of them are yours, love, and He dissipates silently behind the window again.

Sorry to disappoint, but oblivion is hers too, our dark fruit, our black hole.

It is the devil's pet and God's last resort.

4.

It is night, and you are gone, off on some pale ambition,

some midnight quest for minimum-wage.

I flick a lamp on and rise to my feet, longing for oblivion with you once more.

The day passed by in fleeting drops of recognition.

We were in our own dazes, a trance, a sundance worshipping only each other.

In your absence, I, at a loss for what to do, step outside my door and stand underneath a torn, indigo patch of sky.

No moon tonight, the clouds are playing chase with each other across this yawning sky.

What is the sound of one hand clapping?

I ponder this alone.

It is the same soundless sound the moon makes when it nightly swings about a planet blue with tears, and swarming with Armageddon.

I hear it when I do not listen.

I listen to it as a deaf man under the water.

You are my soundless sound; ethereal, a hidden undercurrent, a soul cry.

You are the blood of the poet.

Nightly, the poet bleeds.

He bleeds oblivion.

He bleeds the soundless sound.

He bleeds a soul cry.

He bleeds sunlight cloaked in velvet.

He bleeds hidden prophecy.

He bleeds more than love.

More than life.

He bleeds the echoes of God.

He bleeds the ghost in the machine.

He bleeds paper and ink, and metaphors unseen,

underneath it all like plasma.

The poet bleeds.

The poet is blood.

The poet flows out his spirit in blood.

You are that spirit.

The poet bleeds you.

Open Mic.

the music is sharp and loud,

and the piano shrieks while women laugh.

he walks up to the stage, drunk and
angry,

and the music dies down,

and he grabs that mic as if it were his
wife,

and he puts his lips against her nice
and close,

and he whispers "ssssshhhhhh" and the
audience dies down,

and he lets it get real quiet, as he
focuses on the bartender,

marie, who cut him off and called him an
asshole.

and he catches her eye, and she stops
pouring drinks,

and they look at each other a long
moment like enemy spouses on christmas,

and he takes a deep breath, and the
crowd prepares itself for bad singing,

and at the top of his cancerous lungs,
he yells, "FUUUUUCK YOUUUUU
MARIEEEEE!!!"

and people grab at their bleeding ears
and shoot furious eyes up at him,

and the mic shrieks to a deafening
pitch,

as he swats it down like it was his
wife,

and the big man pulls him off stage,

fighting and screaming and clawing and
cussing like a madman.

and as the next act apologetically picks
the mic up,

hissing and wailing, he stumbles over to
the bar,

steals someone's whiskey,

downs it and starts a fight.

and somewhere in the crunching bloody
boozy mess of it all,

he's laughing his head off, plowing some
guy's head into a wooden table,

and loving the fact that he's still
alive enough to bleed and fight and
scream and drink,

while his head is still ringing with the
gunshots and death cries of war.

Zealots.

we ignored the guides of justice and
trekked,

onward without their foolish advisory,

through the snows of ignorance and
dissent,

to the grand castle of bigotry,

where the moat's filled with intolerant
acid,

and the drawbridge is biased and wary.

and ne'er had we seen such monuments,

to monsters of men, and hatred's army,

if any of us zealots dared to repent,

we were sentenced to a dungeon's
scenery,

which reeked of genocidal detriment,

and the bones of undead slavery.

Intoxication.

it's like being drunk and hungover at
the same time,

this thing.

it's all there,

the giddiness,

the pain,

the loss of control,

the loss of memory,

the wonderment at the mundane,

the agony of poison trying to get out,

the spilling of alcohol,

the sloshing of vomit,

the tendency to want more,

the thought to never do it again,

the passion,

the regret,

the love of lighted stages,

the fear of the sun,

the loving of anyone,

the hating of everyone,

the annoying idiocy,

the tortured genius,

the crying,

the crying,

(in this line of work, there is much crying,)

the arrogance,

the self-loathing,

the openness,

the reclusion,

the making of weird calls,

the lack of contact,

the arguments,

the apologies...

yes, it's just like that,

and sometimes not quite,

this writing thing.

and just like alcohol,

it's either killing me,

or keeping me alive.

For Josh Weir,

who helped to inspire this.
Love you man.

How To Write.

He asked me how I could write so well,

and while I could have gone on about
technique and style,

rhyme scheme, and all the books I'd
read, I didn't.

I just gave him the one metaphor that
was more than metaphor,

something real, something he would not
forget,

something he might understand on a base
level, but yet still never fully
comprehend.

I took my razor blade from its sheath,
tore a page from my notebook, and stood
tall.

I sliced my arm right down the middle, a
shallow but substantial cut.

I bled on the page for a full thirty
seconds, until it was covered.

He said, "Ok, I get it. I get the
analogy. Hey, you can stop now."

I kept on bleeding.

Then I began to cry, in low guttural
sobs that were just as real.

He said, "What's wrong? Are you hurt? Do you need a napkin?"

Then I let forth a primal scream that shattered the silence and modesty of the room.

As I screamed, I began tearing the wet, bloody page into pieces.

He was so taken aback, he stood off to the side, eyeing me like I was a madman.

I sat down and wiped my eyes. I smiled and took a breath.

I handed him the torn pieces of my bloody and tear-stained page,

wiping the blood from my arm with my other hand.

I said, "That's how.

Why, how do you write?"

Cruel Winter.

It was a cruel winter in a harsh, dry
land,

I walked with the Kronosians hand in
hand,

across deserts of ice, and white snowy
plains,

to places where it hails, but it seldom
rains.

We took shelter in the rocks of the
Hypnossian Hills,

and they made fires that never danced,
but seemed to stand still.

And I watched as they mixed herbs into a
fine grey paste,

and the eldest, who looked ancient,
didn't let it go to waste.

He ate it all up, and smiled as he fell
asleep,

and they covered him in blankets, and
called over to me.

They gestured for me to pray over his
body with care,

so I took a deep breath, and I said a
small prayer.

Then they lifted and tossed him up into the fire,

and they threw sticks all upon him; a funeral pyre.

And I sat there bewildered, catching tears in my hand,

Oh, what a cruel, cruel winter in this harsh, dry land.

I Am Not A Writer.

i am not a writer,
just a lost man in the desert,
making compasses out of question marks.

i am not a writer,
just a traveler too broke to travel,
who still owns a million postcards.

i am not a writer,
just a star yearning to be seen,
burning itself out until it explodes.

i am not a writer,
just a song no one plays,
but everyone knows the words to.

i am not a writer,
just a peasant who walks like a prince,
and loves like a god.

i am not a writer,

just a man who turns his pain into,

the beautiful beast you see now.

i am not a writer,

just a flicker of real darkness,

in a world of illusionary light.

i am not a writer,

just a dying man wondering why

life is not lived by the living.

i am not a writer,

just an artist without brushes,

writhing around on a canvas of paper.

i am not a writer,

just a ghost haunting graveyards

created by monsters of war.

i am not a writer,

just a fighter pinned down by disease,

who still won't stop swinging.

i am not a writer,

just a whisper twisting in chaos,

tirelessly uttering one word: "hope."

Heroes.

i will never be honest,

because a lie hides the filth i am,

and the trouble i am in.

i will always lie,

when the secret is too big to be toyed
with,

when my loyalties belong to someone
other than you,

when i need the attention lies can
bring.

i will always be a hero in someone's
eyes,

and a villain in at least one person's
heart.

that one person, therefore, must be
destroyed.

i will make my friends hate you,

i will forget why i loved you,

i will demonize you,

i will be honest where honesty suits me,

and i will never give you credit for
shit.

don't meet your heroes.

we're all liars.

we're heroes, in fact, because we're the best at it.

we're your heroes because our lies seem prettier than yours.

really, they're just more disgusting.

i will never be honest, save for the magnifying glass.

this is how i magnify myself to you.

this is how i warn you.

i am alive, and i fight like hell to stay that way,

but anyone would, as anyone should,

and that does not make me a hero.

the illusion of heroism is made by survival despite adversity,

grace under pressure, patience in hell,

walking out of the fire.

we who can do this are no more than you.

we have just decided to embellish.

we have conspired to be inspirational.

we have survived because we must keep the lie alive.

trust me, don't trust us.

we are trickster gods donning angel
wings,

remaining humble so that they may have
decent idols,

remaining alive because they must have
tangible hope,

remaining heroes because they need the
eternal myth.

because otherwise, we just live in a
world of ungrateful mortals,

liars,

thieves,

rapists,

murderers,

madmen,

pedophiles,

racists,

homophobes,

and other degenerate humanoids.

we are persistent in the face of death,
not brave.

we lie about the heights and depths and
widths of our struggle.

we will never be honest.

keep us in the fire,

the hospital,

the crash,

the hurricane,

the war.

maybe more pain will make us real.

but unless we die, and quite possibly
even then,

we will continue to have our dicks
sucked by the people, and for the
people,

as they make our statues out of the
melted gold from all of their jewelry,

all of their hopes,

all of their dreams,

and all of their prayers.

thanks, we really appreciate it, we
really do.

but if i may give you any advice,

keep it all for yourselves,

and put your faith in you.

i don't care if you lie to me, be your
own hero,

we were heroes to ourselves years before
a little trouble made us heroes to you.

we'll be heroes to ourselves forever,

and for no reason, i might add,

other than, simply, our unrelenting
egotism.

throw yourselves a parade,

use your minds,

and be heroic together by advancing us
as a species,

instead of worshipping a new
reincarnation of the sun.

i'm full of shit, even if my scars are
real.

just because my story seems miraculous,

doesn't make me a saint.

my scar is the best weapon i have,

because you're all wounded at the heart
from the moment you see it,

and then i've got you, and then i win.

i will never be honest,

because a lie hides the filth i am,

and the trouble i am in.

truth is, you are all in trouble,

and the only real hero that can save
you,

is you. no lie.

there's nothing bigger.

there's nothing bigger than the fear of
burning,

in the middle of the night, when you
can't sleep,

and you're so hot that you wish you
could fling off your skin,

and lie naked in bed, just searing
flesh, and baked brittle bones.

there's nothing bigger than your room in
the darkness,

when you're standing at the doorway
after switching off the light,

and you've forgotten where your bed is,

or where the dead weight of some fine
young mexican chick named marisol is
lying,

flat on her back like a tortilla, hands
at her sides,

like a corpse that's too pretty to bury,

so you wanna wrap her up like a burrito.

there's nothing bigger than the madness
that gestates and burns inside you,

when it's 2:30 in the morning and you're
up raping muse after muse,

and the dogs won't stop barking,

and you break the pen you borrowed from
the indian at the front desk.

because you can't write a suicide note
in blood,

believe me, i've tried.

i can't get past the first sentence
without passing out like a pussy,

but i'm long-winded anyway.

there's nothing bigger than the pain in
your chest,

when the stress becomes a physical
entity,

and that motherfucker pounds on you,

and stabs you,

and whales on you like you fucked his
mother while he was away at grad school.

and the panic begins in the crowd
mentality as you grab your chest,

insisting that this is not a heart
attack,

and please don't call 911 until i'm sure
it won't go away.

there's nothing bigger than the shit i
took last wednesday,

i swear to god,

when i ate my weight in crawfish and
shrimp,

and pooped out a whole fucking cajun,

right there in the handicapped bathroom!

oh man did ya smell dat....poo-yee!

i got de freesôns from that un, i did!

there's nothing bigger than my ego after
i trick some poor bastard into reading
my work to me,

while i sit contemplating jerking off
and further editing.

i usually just jerk off.

there's nothing bigger than god when god
is in the belly of yet another friday
whore,

and all i'm trying to do is shake his
hand,

or blind him with the promise of a
future generation of asshole poets like
myself.

there's nothing bigger than hyperbole,

when you stretch it halfway to the moon,

put mt. everest in it,

and fire it like a slingshot straight at
your ex wife's house,

hoping to god that as it burns on
reentry, it melts every bit of snow,

and sharpens the tip of the mountain,

so that it kills her, manuel, and the
entire fucking housing project in the
worst way possible.

there's nothing bigger than the fear of
death,

even as i'm trying to achieve it,

because there's nothing left to say once
you die,

and i never run out of things to say,

and god help the world should i ever
stop writing this bullshit down,

and god help you all should i be too
stubborn to die,

because that also means i'll be too
stubborn to be allowed to live,

and then the only thing to do will be
the only thing i've wanted,

and even when i get what i want,

i'll still want more.

yes, there's nothing bigger than
wanting,

in fact, it's the biggest thing,

because even god and death want more,

and it always gets bigger and bigger,

and there will never be an end to what
you can have,

or what you can do,

or what you can write,

if you just keep dreaming.

but we're all dreaming if we think we
can have any of it,

which makes the wanting as infinite as
the distance between us and what we
truly desire,

and if all i really want is a fine death
somewhere within the space of a book
deal and a good screw,

then i'll live forever, and want for
nothing more,

and there's nothing bigger than that.

god's boy.

it was raining.

god got home sopping wet, and closed the door.

he set his books down on the table with a thump, and looked up.

something was burning, he could smell it.

he flicked on the light.

"lucy? show yourself. i know you're there."

she stepped into sight from the darkness.

"you look like a wet dog," she said, smiling.

"what do you want? i have put up with too much today to have to deal with you too."

she played with her hair and giggled.

"i want the boy."

god tossed his jacket on the chair and summoned himself a drink.

"you want anything to drink?"

satan plopped herself down on god's recliner and leaned back,

stretching like an old cat.

"nah, i'm good. how's j?"

god downed a swig of heaven's finest dark brew,

which had been stored away in the cellar since peyton randolph was president.

"he's in his workshop building god kn....he's building a bookshelf.

you can't have the boy, lucy. you can influence him, you can whisper to him,

but that boy is mine, and you can't have him."

satan leaned forward in the recliner, determined.

"why do you want him so much? have you read what he's written?

have you seen what he's done?"

god walked over to satan as she crossed her legs.

"get out of my chair."

satan uncrossed her legs, stood, and walked over to a stool, sitting down with a smirk.

god sat down and sighed.

"it doesn't matter, lucy. just because
he's not a goody two-shoes,

or has his own demons doesn't mean i
can't use him.

you of all people should understand
that. he can write what he wants. i need
him.

his words are destined to turn the tide
in our battle. you know that.

he doesn't have to be a christian or
even religious to do that.

as long as he doesn't choose you in the
end, he will always be mine."

satan stood and grimaced, hating having
to hear the truth.

"he speaks blasphemy! he's lied,
cheated, stolen, deceived,

and his writing speaks of his contempt
for you and even his disbelief in your
son!"

god smiled.

"shouldn't you be happy about that? look
at paul.

he used to hate me with a passion back
when he was saul.

he doesn't start out loving me, and he
doesn't have to.

he doesn't have to believe anything
right now,

i'm still working on him, molding him.

a lump of clay has no eyes to see its
maker until they are fully made! "

satan sat back down, humbled by god's
wisdom,

and hating the fact that god could still
do that to her, even now.

"well i hope you mold him something
useful,

because i'm gonna continue to make his
life a living hell!

i'll make sure he hates you, even when
his eyes are open!

his life will be a hell he cannot
escape, and just when he's about to give
up,

i will be there, and i will sway him to
our side.

i will promise him all the books in the
world, all the literary acclaim, all the
fame,

and all the glory and he will not be
able to refuse,

because unlike you, i will actually give
those things to him! ! ! "

god took another big swig and sat it
down.

he laid back in his chair and looked at
satan with those big light blue eyes.

"i don't need to give all that to him.
it wouldn't mean a thing if i did.

he has to earn those things. and he
will, you'll see."

suddenly, a door opened and shut, and
from his workshop emerged j,

sweaty and covered in wood shavings.

he walked past satan like she wasn't
even there, and grabbed a bottled water
from the fridge.

he turned around and looked at both his
father and satan, taking a drink of his
water.

"awww, don't tell me you guys are
fighting again."

he turned his eyes to lucy and grinned,
"are you and dad gonna get a divorce?"

j chuckled to himself as satan just
hissed and turned to face god again.

"i hate that kid."

god beamed at an angry lucy, "that's my
boy."

he turned to jesus, "so how's it coming along?"

j grabbed a stool of his own and sat.

"pretty good. i'm surprised you guys can't hear me hammering in here.

well, not really, i guess, since you can soundproof, but still. so is she after...?"

j broke his sentence and took a drink, already knowing the answer.

"yep. but it's not working."

he smiled at lucy,

who was getting more and more nervous having both of them in the same room as her.

she could stand one, but this was getting to be a bit too much spiritual intensity.

"at least dove isn't here," satan muttered under her breath.

god's eyes flickered up, and she knew he'd heard it.

she looked at j and smiled, "actually, j, i could hear the hammering.

you sure you don't need a...hand? i could nail some things to you, whoops, i mean, for you."

j smiled ear to ear, "you just couldn't resist huh? that's ok, satan. i forgive you."

chills went down satan's back, and her clothes started smoking.

"maybe it's you who needs help though, with your little fire pit?

maybe i should help you secure that thing. gotta be careful about that.

you wouldn't want anyone else busting outta hell intent on revenge, huh?"

god stood. "that's enough, you two.

you're like backseat children when you get into the puns and what not."

he smiled to himself, and went over to satan and patted her on her shoulder,

which was so hot, that the imprint of his hand was burned onto her shirt.

"you know, lucy, you might as well stop trying.

you know as well as i do that since it's HIS free will that decides,

so there's no point in you coming here to plea for him. go home.

you have so much going on in the world that i'm surprised you could find the time to stop in."

satan stood up, knocking his hand away, and went to the fridge.

she grabbed a bottled water and poured it onto herself.

the steam emanated from her body with a snakelike hiss and rose high in the air.

"and you know that if i can't have his heart, i'll take his life!

this is not another job deal, you won that bet. i can kill this one."

god laughed, "then he's mine by default."

"but his words will be lost!"

god stepped forward, "to earth, but not to heaven.

as long as he's mine, his words can make a difference in the battle.

people will need his words of hope when armaggedon hits,

and i'll make sure they'll have them, one way or another."

satan's fist clenched as the bottle melted, "then i'll make him kill himself! he will be mine then!"

j stepped between the two, "he's too strong for that. you can try, but you will not succeed."

god sat back down and took one final gulp of his brew, "he's right. go home, lucy. this is pointless."

satan smiled, "this isn't over. what do you see in that little pipsqueak anyway?

what good will his words do in the middle of the hell that will be unleashed?

why waste your time saving a measly poet?"

god stood and spoke a microphone into being, and shouted into it, as his words shook the house,

"BECAUSE I AM THE VERY FIRST POET,

AND THEY TOO WIELD THE VERY POWER OF CREATION!!!"

god dropped the mic.

dishes fell and broke, and satan held onto the door for dear life until the house stopped shaking.

j stood up, "dad! if you have to do that, do it outside!

my tools and nails are probably all over the workshop floor."

god turned to his son. "not anymore," he said, winking.

lucy nervously fiddled with the doorknob, "well, i'll find a way to influence him, you can be sure.

poet or no poet, he will belong to me."

turning her eyes to j, she grinned an evil grin and said, "nail you later jesus. i'm out."

satan ran back to her car, as the rain fell, steaming as it hit her.

the door creaked shut, and god instantly fixed the dishes and restored them to their proper places.

god sat back down and turned on the news.

"on tuesday, republicans joined forces to declare their opposition

to a constitutional amendment supporting same-sex marriage..."

god sighed and turned to j, whose hand was already on the workshop door.

"see this? oh, she's definitely been busy."

j opened the door to his workshop and looked proudly at his finished bookshelf.

"that's okay, dad, because so are we. i'll see you at dinner. love you."

"remember, michael will be here at seven with the lambchops. i love you too, son."

j closed the workshop door, rolling up his sleeves and licking his lips.

"mmmm, lambchops! "

the rain stopped suddenly, and a beam of light rose in the window, and shone in god's eyes.

god flipped through the seemingly unending channels and shook his head.

"we sure do have a lot of work to do. just hold tight, kid. we'll see you through."

meanwhile, somewhere on earth, a skinny poet is finishing up another piece.

"and while i know there is a lot of work to do, if i can just hold tight, he will see me through."

he looks up with a hopeful smile, and notices the rain has stopped.

the sun shines on him, and he looks proudly at his finished work, and signs it.

split knee promises.
(a love letter to rock bottom.)

have you ever made split knee promises?

the gravel at rock bottom swells the
feet,

and you find yourself looking for the up
elevator.

here, god's name is repeated in earnest
more than any church.

here is where the rubber would meet the
road,

if there were any rubber left, and the
road led anywhere.

have you ever felt like you would give a
blow-job for a good sandwich?

have you ever been robbed of the luxury
of choice?

have you ever rubbed the dirt in your
wounds because it's all you have?

have you ever been healed by another
kind of sickness?

headphones here become sacred, no matter
what you use them for.

you can find hidden treasure in the back
of your pantry,

once all the other canned goods are gone.

a big can of peaches can make you cry.

who knew eating by candlelight can be so goddamned unromantic?

you lie on a towel in an open field at 1:30 am,

and listen for the crickets to tell you the secret of happiness.

a certain kind of sufficiency is maintained when the distractions die off.

you don't see it as settling once you realize what you still have when you seem to have nothing.

you begin to long for these once-forfeited walks with god.

you begin to forget about the power bill in the presence of true power.

you awaken on the reality of your wounds.

what once was painful and bothersome becomes viewed

as the only entryway to a body numb to all the other signs.

once you see that, you begin to wonder what got in, and why.

god swims in the blood, and resets the fire.

you become grateful and hungry for more life.

have you ever thanked god for rock bottom?

the only way to look is up, and the only way out is to climb.

he wants you stronger.

he wants to remind you of what living is.

he wants more than split knee promises.

he wants the results that healing can bring.

he wants you back from yourself,

from your demons,

from the world.

there is no up elevator,

only the stairs you carve out, step by step.

if you want out, you'll get out.

if he wants you to wake up,

he'll shake you.

if he wants you to seek him,

he'll hide the light so you can find him
in the darkness.

and in doing so,

you will find yourself,

and shine once more.

America, I.

America, I am a law-abiding citizen in
this land of the lawless.

America, I am shackled to the image of
freedom.

America, I see your flags waving, but
the war isn't over.

America, I see men on patrol but I do
not feel safe.

America, I celebrate your independence
day while in invisible chains.

America, I sing God bless America, while
you damn God with your actions.

America, I see now that your primary
export is hypocrisy.

America, I see the poor on streets, and the innocent in prisons, and I know this was not the dream.

America, I see your Constitution being destroyed to disenfranchise the people it was meant to protect.

America, I am allowed the freedom of speech for now, but even a caged bird can sing.

America, I am not so blinded by your distractions that I fail to see my rights being taken away.

America, I know that soon, you will silence me, for "my own good."

America, I know that soon you will monitor my every action, for "my safety."

America, I know that soon you will decide what I eat and where I go, for "my convenience."

America, I know that soon all of my
assets will be seized, for "taxes owed."

America, I know that soon we'll be
enslaved in our own homes, here in "the
land of the free."

America, I see you for what you're
becoming, but you underestimate the
tenacity of your people.

America, I am awake and aware and will
fight for my rights and the rights of
others,

America, I will never give up on making
you a better place for the next
generation.

America, I still love you, but things
must change, and they must change now.

The Truth About Walls.

she is as tough as nails, yet vulnerable
like roses,

like an impenetrable wall that kept all
attackers at bay during the day,

but reeled every night from the full
force of every blow,

her tears crumbling down between the
cracks of her stony armor.

she was my protector, challenging all
comers,

she was my heart, asking the mirror each
night if someone could love her without
being deflected,

without attacking her themselves and
forcing her to be a wall again.

she was sister moon, reflecting the
awesome power of the sun in the middle
of the night,

hovering above anyone who would dare
make another crater in her gray flesh.

sometimes i pray that a knight would
come riding for her, wearing no armor,

naked and free, vulnerable, yet very
strong.

i would ask him to stand at the wall,
gently walk up to it, and place roses in
the cracks, in the holes.

i would ask him to kiss the wall in true
earnest and love,

and prove himself a man by the measure
of his actions.

as she turns back to herself, as the
moon touches earth, as the wall crumbles
away,

i see her tracing the horizon of his
scars, filling the holes in his chest
with her hands.

and maybe for once, someone could
protect her, and she would be loved,

and be able to wash the gray of stone
away, and just be a woman.

his woman.

forever, babe.

the persistence of past memories
guarantees this night be spent awake,

i just want you to know, that babe, it's
no mistake that we are together,

forever's not a love song, but a team
effort to pull through hell,

love each other on earth, and achieve
heaven,

all while trying not to kill each other
or ourselves.

i remember how we met,

nervously in a fast food restaurant,

laptop monitors touched and guarded us
from each other until we both felt safe.

the dates we went on were cheap and fun,
and we still follow suit.

i remember the moment i gave in and fell
for you,

in line at the galleria, as you told me
things about yourself that mirrored my
fears and thoughts.

how long had i fought to resurrect the
dead heart inside me,

beaten down by years of bad family and old relationships?

it had been too long, but you made me feel alive again, and ever since,

we've bonded and joined in our struggles,

both the mountain i was facing, as well as your many uphill battles.

and if we tarry too long, we hear failure rattle and hiss behind us,

reminding us that while we are soulmates, it is our hearts and lives at stake here.

and now a year and five months later, we're married, free, and in another state.

man we pulled it together so many times to escape, but my memory rapes me,

holds me down and makes me see things i wish i could forget.

yet, thank god you were there every time, and every pain that was mine was yours too,

and because of you, baby, i pulled through.

you're my everything, protector,
guardian angel, husband too, and i love
you more each day,

for the way you are there when i break.

oh, for heaven's sake, i'm crying, not
griping but while typing this, my heart
leaps up,

and my eyes mist, you are the best, and
every kiss was true from day one, and
will be to the last.

we feel each other's pain, and when we
gain the victory,

whether it's in jesus' name or the
universes refrain of another soul
reclaimed,

i don't know what to believe in, but you
give me such faith.

and i'm sorry for the danger of constant
sorrow when i'm sick,

and for the anger that i show when i'm
tired and wanna quit,

but my mind is made, heart is repaid for
all the kindness it ever showed
unrequited,

and i fight again, you make me want to
win.

and don't worry about the way the words
come out of your mouth,

i see the thought, the love, the power
behind your eyes,

that we both recognize but your tongue
can't decide on.

it's ok, i get twisted up too, even now,
i'm between a rhyme and a hard place,

and i just want out, but that hard place
toughens me, makes my words sure,

makes my heart pure when the world's
bootprints are more than it can handle.

you are my candle, you are my healer,
you know me deeper,

i'd be lying next to you now, but the
words need this paperless paper,

to record what the lord has done.

yes, baby, i said it, i'm not afraid of
our god, don't you ever forget it,

and i don't hate his people, just the
hypocrisy,

and i cringed with each steeple until
you showed me,

that there is power in the blood, even
if i doubt the body,

and i want to believe, and even when my faith is shoddy,

i see him in you, and i see him full well,

and if he exists, then he knows why i believed in hell but little else.

well, that's it, but you changed all of that, and you're changing me still,

if i'd shut up and lie back, and let god handle my worries, while you handle my heart,

babe without you, i swear i'd fall the ever-loving fuck apart,

and oh god here i go, crying again, i can hear it,

my heart leaping in joy, that must be the holy spirit.

and as these tears hit the keyboard, i just want you to know,

that when you wake up tomorrow, i'll tell you i love you so,

fuck this poem, fuck rhyme, why i gotta do that all the time?

it's instinctive, it stinks and i'm just trying to say that i love you, i love you,

that's all there is in me, and i'm
coming soon to lie next to you, me and
my memory.

i sit here and remember all the hard
times we had, but look at us now baby,

my momma'd be so mad and i love that!
fuck her, she doesn't deserve a line
here.

this space is reserved for the one i
hold dear, cause you hold me right here,

and i point to my chest, where the pain
can send me reeling as you hold me and
say rest,

as you worry, and do all you can to stop
the pain,

but the reason my chest hurts is my
heart can't contain all this love,

look, i'm ranting, i should put a line
break,

oh, right here and say fuck it, i love
you, randy, forever babe.

when i open my notebook.

when i open my notebook, i don't see
words.

i see days and pain and smudges of ink
where words used to be,

because i was crying faster than i could
write.

i see ideas, i see landscapes, i see a
trauma ward in some dark lonely
hospital,

where the only doctor is a pen,

and the only medicine is reliving the
trauma until you're too calloused to
fear it,

and too numb to weep for it.

i see growing pains, stages, ages, dead
dreams and unfinished hopes.

i see thoughts quivering with potential,
i see emotions standing naked,

too raw to be made eloquent, too painful
to be articulated.

i see my soul through a twisted mirror
of self.

i see a soulless twisted world more
clearly.

i see hospital beds, and foster homes,
and highways and hedges missions,

and crack houses, and drug addicts, and
liars, and thieves, and my mother,

the minotaur of that labyrinth of
instability and fear.

i see the dead clawing their way back to
whisper to me.

i see betrayal by media, citizen, and
government.

i see the puppet show of politics, and
delusions as grand as a thousand three-
ring circuses,

and religious terror, and
indoctrination, and screaming fights
against god.

i see my soul piece by piece, i see a
broken heart,

and a trust damaged beyond repair.

i see characters and real people, i see
jesus and mythology,

i see a secret history, and a dystopian
future.

i see a rainbow flag more tattered than
old glory.

i see villains and bullies, phobias and
crushing anxieties,

demons and angels, and creatures i
cannot describe.

i see you, i see crowds, i see my name
in lights,

i see my name on an asylum door, i see
my name on a headstone.

i see poets and singers, dancers and
artists, i see unsung heroes,

and forgotten deities.

i see an inverted reflection of a dying
world.

i see the horribly beautiful, the
strangely wonderful,

the brave, the broken, the cripples, and
the fighters.

i see love defeating hate in all her
glorious splendor and might.

i see so much more than words when i
open my notebook.

i see a life unwritten, waiting for me
to write it,

as it writhes invisibly between the
lines of blank paper.

i listen to the voices in my head, and i
proceed to tell their stories,

as i see through their eyes.

i hear them crying out to me, and i cry with them.

the ink runs with my tears, and stains each tale with the mark of bards and prophets.

i carry all of this and more, in a composition notebook,

which is composed of universes and populations produced by pain, but given life by love.

when i open my notebook, i don't see words.

i see existence becoming, and reality bending to the will of poets like myself.

i become the creator, the shaman, the scribe.

i become a greater version of myself,

because what i see the most is my own heart, bleeding with love and perseverance,

slowly growing stronger to facilitate the new me,

which is steadily being created with every single stroke of my powerful pen.

The Charge of The Lighthouse.

I woke up with self-doubt, the gasoline
of fear.

This is how it starts:

I am afraid because I don't think I can.

I am afraid I am wrong and leading you
in the wrong direction.

I am afraid I am handling things in the
wrong way.

I am afraid I want all the wrong things
for myself.

I'm not sure what I do matters, even
with the evidence of doing right.

I feel like some of this comes from some
strange outsider beyond the walls of
myself, like an attacker at the castle
wall.

When I am confident, there is nothing
that compares with me.

I am beautiful, and furthermore, and
even more important, I AM STRONG.

I feel good, I know what I'm doing, I
can see the light around myself, as if I
stood in a lighthouse and looked out at
the beam of light which is savior to so
many in the darkness.

Does a lighthouse have doubts about its long monotonous ever-sweeping circle?

Does it ever doubt that it can find anyone out there in all that stormy darkness?

Does it start each morning in the stinging cold wondering if its masters will forget to light that spark?

We are lucky we can light our own, but this self-doubt is like water on the wick.

When that spark is lit, when I am aware of every fiber of my being lighting up with this power, I don't feel so helpless and broken anymore.

I feel whole when others are found in my light.

I know who that lighthouse was and still is for me, and she can also fall prey to self-doubt and second guessing herself.

But she lead me in from the dark, and has continued to be a source of light and love for me.

I crashed into a few rocks on the way home, simply due to fate, and my own doubts and distractions.

I came home broken, but I'm here, and despite all the questions and pain she has, she repairs me and prepares me to go back out into the deep.

She should know that when she lights up, from an outside perspective, there is no greater force.

She is a tower, she is a warrior, she is a force of nature.

Is this what others see in me when I am on?

If so, than there is no reason to doubt myself.

I go with my first instinct, I trust the universe knows what it's doing with and through me, I don't subscribe to my own fear, which would be my excuse NOT TO do what I am meant to: SHINE.

If I falter, I get back up. Too many people depend on me, and I have to be there, present within myself to light that wick.

Fear not the monotony or the darkness.

I help people. I mend broken boats.

I send them back out into the deep to serve the purpose they were given.

I shine and I seek you out.

Look for me.

I'll be the second-brightest, second-farthest reaching light in the western sky.

Trumped only by the stars, which hover above us so very far away, and shine in a more eternal darkness, devoid of doubt or fear.

So brightly did they shine that they themselves are long gone, but their light is still seen by us, guiding us home, and teaching us much about our amazing potential to shine.

I want to shine so brightly and for so long that even when I'm gone, you can STILL see my light, and be guided home by it.

There is no room in this lighthouse for fear or doubt.

There is only room for light. So shine. Such is the charge of the lighthouse.

And I accept, by first accepting myself, and loving myself, and secondly, by letting the power of that action spark a great light in myself.

I can only hope you do the same.

Shine brightly, and never let the darkness in.

I Am Ready. (Excelsior!)

Let me begin this by stating something:

happiness is the fuel of despair.

The precursor to a new attack. The catalyst for destructive change for constructive growth.

A smile is the thunderclap loosing an avalanche of problems.

It's good for you, but be prepared.

It's like one must wear a life jacket especially during smooth sailing.

The beating of a contented heart is the shattering of a new barrier holding back the demons.

They prey on the bliss like vultures around a dead carcass.

They cannot love the suffering, because they are incapable of such an emotion.

And because they ARE the suffering.

Yet constant sadness still is not the answer.

It's bad for your soul.

It seems that even when we do not, it is our souls, or something inside us that craves the fevered heartbeats of worry, thrives upon the pain, is most happy within the raging of the battle, where life is most precarious, and the threat of death makes you come alive even more.

Much like a daredevil or a thrill seeker, it is the rush that your soul gets from danger and the persistence it shows during pain, that it feeds on the most.

But do not despair, within your desperation is the key to an untouchable and immortal happiness.

That you are here, fighting, struggling, against all odds, while your heart paces faster to keep up, and your soul cheers you on as you create and find solutions within a sea of problems.

That you are alive enough to WANT to push through the madness and anger, to something better, even if it too, will inevitably crumble somewhere along the way.

That you dream the impossible dream, know the stars are too distant and dangerous, and climb upward anyway, persistent, insistent, courageously battling your way up towards the light.

And so, in my despair and anger, and in my delicious happiness evermore so, I rage anyway, knowing that I will, I must lose some battles, nay most.

Knowing that the goal is not truly bliss in this life, but the next, while fighting for as much of it as you can find and create while you are here.

And when I say you make me happy, I do not mean you beset these monsters on all sides of me on purpose.

Your love brings me joy, damn the consequences.

Maybe this is why we hurt the ones we love the most, even though we don't intend to.

Because in giving the gift we meant to give, we give another: that of an adventure for your loved one.

A challenge that is unavoidable.

A potential victory.

An inevitable defeat that will teach them so much more than love ever could.

I love you. I wish nothing but love upon you.

But I also hope you become brave, patient, wiser.

I hope you win. I hope your battles are for something greater than yourself.

I know you'll one day win the whole damn war.

I know that then, finally and eternally, you'll be happy.

The demons and monsters will fall away and die, like old diseased flesh that once served a purpose for you.

And those conquered mountains will turn into a colossal pile of treasures, all of them for you.

I know you'll do fine. I'll help you out in the midst of your battles when I can.

I will pray for strength and courage for all of us.

And all those things we learned and gained along the way all this time, will be somehow of use to you there, in the great ever after.

God will see to it nothing you accomplished is wasted.

Perhaps you were being prepared for the next great adventure, a final battle.

Who knows?

I say enjoy the happiness while it lasts, and learn something from the hard times.

Bask in the light, and take something of value from the darkness.

Become greater than you are, and do it all with love. I salute you, brave soldier.

Now the time has come to shed our skin, to take up arms, to transcend the pain and enter a higher form, a loftier thought path, a humbler outlook, a stronger vision, a more relentless compassion, a tougher heart, a wiser mind, and a better soul.

I love you and want nothing but the best for you, as well as I love myself and want the best for myself.

But just remember what The Rolling Stones said: "You can't always get what you want, but if you try sometimes, you just might find, YOU GET WHAT YOU NEED."

Onward and upward.

I am ready. Excelsior!

battleground.

this is supposed to be yet another poem
to quell the pain,

to turn it into glory,

to make it make sense,

to rise above it,

to be inspirational by being happy
despite it, but not today.

today, i'm a soldier in a battle whose
only silver lining is seen once it's
over.

there is no philosophy or clarity to be
had in the middle of the battle,

there is only pain, and the need to
fight,

and the desire to stay alive to see that
silver lining again.

there is no wit, there is no humor, and
there is very little wisdom.

there is only pain, and the only wisdom
is surviving it.

there is screaming and curses to god,

and struggles to make it to the bathroom
that destroy your independence and
dignity.

if you want to see my bravery, come back when i'm healing, and i'll show you my scars.

right now, all i have to show you are open wounds and a faith that,

no matter how many times you rebuild it in your interim, is always shattered again.

you don't want to see the things a soldier goes through,

or has to do in order to come back home.

so write me as much as you want, and wait for me to return to myself.

and always expect to say goodbye one more time.

because i'll always be dragged back, and i'll always get wounded again,

and just in case this time is my last battle, and your last goodbye,

i'll always remember you as the silver lining i could never see until the smoke cleared, and the pain faded.

thanks for being the reason i will always come back home.

the little deaths.

it's the little deaths i die with you
that make me love you:

the reluctant concessions,

the not-so-gracious defeats,

the compromises,

the forgone prizes,

the tolerated temper-tantrums,

the innocent one apologizing,

the threat of losing you, and
consequently, everything,

the reality of forever, and ever, and
ever,

the promise of no promises,

the dedication to forgiveness when i
deserve punishment,

the parable without the preacher,

the refusal of leverage,

the little deals we make, and break,

the nightmares we need,

the dreams we don't feed,

the mistakes you make that anger me so
because they mirror my own,

the having to settle for less,

the helpless giving,

the infernal waiting,

the financial planning,

the destruction of plans,

the disease of impatience,

the acute accusations,

the asinine assumptions,

the frequent interruptions,

the heated fights about nothing of
importance,

the emotional wars we fight on the
inside,

the wishing without logic,

the hoping without evidence,

the conversations stuck at an impasse,

the furious silences,

the imperfections that plague golden
moments,

and lastly, the ever-selfless love.

it really is these little deaths i die
with you that make me love you so,

and i wanna die again a little each day
with you, for the rest of my life,

until we reach the ageless gates of
eternity, hand-in-hand.

Photo by Desmene Statum

crush.

crush me between your fingers, until i cry out, until i submit,

until i'm almost nothing, and then crush me a little more,

(god i love the way some stars burn for an eternity, with no witness,)

end me, roll everything in me out through the top like a tube of toothpaste, squeeze my disease out and then discard me,

(god i love the way you break bread over my table,)

turn me inside out like a pocket full of lint, and clean me as you see fit, guts and all,

(god i love the way the grass smells the best only after it's cut,)

step on me, grind the dirt in until i'm squished and swallowed by the ground,

(god i love the way the pressure makes a diamond out of a piece of coalthat loved itself just as it was,)

push me down until i can't breathe, and make each breath after it more difficult to accomplish,

(god i love the way the rain feels on my
skin after a bad argument,)

pull me apart until i'm stretched across
your table, screaming for release,

coming clean about every sin, as my arms
and legs extend in agony,

(god i love the way a bruise looks like
a rainbow, and feels like thunder,)

crumple me into a little ball, and let
all of my impurities be pressed out,

do this until i am nothing but humility
and callouses,

(god i love the way this paper cuts me
and heals me at the same damn time.)

the gods can wait.

it is evening, and i lie restless and fearful in my bed.

the disease is closing in on me for the kill, and i'm not ready.

i begin an argument with the empty air.

"i am putting my foot down, the gods can wait."

outside, the silver dollar moon hides itself behind the clouds,

a grinning vault in the sky i cannot escape.

i am reaching for the goal that is not there, i am yearning for the finish line, which from my distance,

looks as if i will break through it as i run, in victory, but in fact, the closer i get,

is slowly becoming a guillotine of wasted accomplishment. first prize is last goodbyes.

"i am putting my foot down, i don't want to go anymore, i'm happy!"

the clouds above me are born and die too quickly to ever have wanted anything else for themselves, and still, there are storms.

"i see it coming, the inspirational
finish, the gaudy ceremony filled with
people who only half-knew me,

and have never read my work.

i have more to live for now, don't do
this, you goddamn gods can wait.

biding is your favorite pastime, besides
smiting, and i am smote enough, just
wait! "

i am being pulled down river, kicking
and screaming and gulping in water
between screams,

as i near the precipice of the fall,
"this was not the plan! " i gurgle on my
way down,

"all i wanted....a simple outing..." and
i am underwater.

suddenly, i am not in my bed or body
anymore, my fearful daydreaming cut
short.

i stand before darkness, and a board of
directors,

but enough redundancy, i have come for
my final appeal.

i look down, and the grooves in the mahogany floor of last chances are those in the shape of knees.

i am to beg for my life, or face oblivion.

there are four of them, and they smell like brimstone and fear, though not their own.

they drink the forfeited tears of the damned, and chuckle to themselves,

as i am forced down by a terribly big unseen hand.

the grooves fit perfectly. two years ago, i was begging to go, and now i beg to stay.

one of them speaks up, "grovel!"

his voice is what a raging bonfire would sound like if it had a tongue and lips.

it crackles and hisses, and if it's meant to be creepy, well fucking done.

i look down again, and in my mind i see the tears of a thousand dead men, wasted here for nothing.

i look up. the gods will not wait. this is my last stand. dramatic music plays in my head, and i am about to give a roaring speech about how I WILL NOT BEG, YOU FUCKING BASTARDS,

but i am awakened by a loud bird chirping outside my window.

it is morning. my chest hurts, and as i wonder if that was a dream,

i can hear the bird chirping something. i listen closely, still rubbing my eyes.

"two more years. chirp! chirp! CHIRP! full of smiting CHIRRRP!!! enjoy, asshole. chirp!"

he flies away. i jump out of bed,

my morning breath reminiscent of those glorious fucking pricks who have spared me!

"THE GODS WILL WAIT!!! smite all you want, dicks, i'll be ready then!"

i put my clothes on, go outside, and tempt the gods with my joy,

free in knowing i have a little more time.

if i have to beg next time, fuck it, i'll beg,

but i'm always coming back to you babe, gods willing.

proof.

(letter to an absent messiah.)

please, for the love of god, show me
your face.

i don't really eat toast,

and i've never paid attention to
bathroom wall art,

but just do whatever it takes to make
yourself known to me.

will i believe?

who knows, but i'll appreciate you
trying to reach out to me.

tonight it would be really cool if you
could call me to the front of the store,
via the cvs speakers above my head.

tonight, things aren't bad and still, i
have worries,

and it'd be nice to finally know if
you're still here or were you ever?

if i just had a sign, (i know, i know
sign of jonah's all i'm getting but
fucking humor me,

that book is crazy,) i would finally be
able to tell him i believe what he does,

and maybe it'd all make sense to me.

but i think too much, and i ask too many
questions,

and i don't really like the idea that my
mind is being controlled by a group of
people

who make money off of peoples spiritual
vulnerabilities.

see what i mean? can i just be
delusional now?

i don't care anymore, i wanna fit in,

i want randy to feel comfortable that i
believe like he does,

even though i know he will love me
forever no matter what.

maybe that's you.

maybe this whole situation is a catalyst
for my perspective to be raised high
enough

and pulled back far enough to be able to
see your face.

but as i've said for years, where's the
assurance?

how do i know you're right? that it all
is true?

and then i think about the horrible
implications

of everything in the bible being dead on,

if not a little mistranslated and misunderstood.

is that really the god we serve?

do you really expect me to be able to live in that kind of a world?

seriously?

and if hell is real, as well as such a god that would even consider punishing the beings he created to be that way forever and ever in the worst way possible,

for things that mean diddly squat in the grand fucking scheme of things,

how could any of us sleep or exist in that world???

a world where god will turn you into salt for looking back,

throw you in hell for being gay,

ask you to kill your son, and then, "sike! test of faith!"

ask his own son to die for a people that hated him, and still do,

except for the ones who love him,

many of whom are crazy religious nuts
responsible for genocide,

refuse to talk to us himself, so he
sends prophets and family members

to help him passively aggressively
deliver his wrath and judgment,

allow a woman to be stoned for adultery,

but force that same woman to marry her
attacker, if raped?

the list could go on forever.

and also, what about the fact that there
are hundreds of gods who came before
him,

who share many of the exact attributes
that made jesus who he was?

is it really just all astrology and
mythology?

because honestly, i am pretty fucking
convinced at this point

that he was contrived to allow the
higher-ups to control us.

are all those religious people, many of
which are nuts anyways,

but many other of which that are good
people at heart,

all delusional sheeple who have no idea
that they have been worshipping

a motherfucking nonexistent build-a-god
for their entire lives?

so somewhere down the line, i have to
accept,

for my own mental sanity, that a lot of
it is either a misinterpreted
translation

of a really old and confusing book, or
that it's all just complete bullshit
flat-out,

and be just confused about what's real
and what's not.

somewhere down the line, i either have
to accept jesus christ as my personal
lord and savior

because it's geographically the thing to
do,

and also because he loved me enough to
die, but not enough to give me proof,

or spend the rest of my life questioning
the meaning of it all,

and always wondering if i'm wrong about
god,

or if we are really all alone out here.

somewhere down the line, i have to say,
okay,

the majority of this country believes in
this guy,

puts his merchandise on everything they
own,

makes music and movies and churches
dedicated to him, and i do not believe
he exists at all,

which should greatly disturb me and my
husband, but in fact, does not.

i want the proof, just like every
agnostic and atheist and undecided
person wants,

that he is in control and wants my best
interests at heart,

but more importantly, that he is
considerate enough to go,

okay, i clearly owe these poor saps an
explanation and should, sometime this
millennia,

just show the fuck up and put a button
on it for good.

i mean, he hung on a cross and died for
me, but he can't show up and hang?

kinda fishy for a guy with all the time
in existence, and the biggest heart
ever.

and if it's a case of his dad not
allowing it, of whom he is a part,

then i have nothing to say about that,
other than,

goddamn i hope there's a good reason
because just by showing up you could
instill global faith,

destroy all the wrong religions and
churches, prevent every war ever,

and solidify public opinion on your
existence and your love for us.

oh, and we can ask you all the questions
we ever wanted to ask you.

the sad ones, the mind-blowing ones,

hell, even the funny ones like can you
make a rock so big even you can't carry
it?

so, just once, even if just a flash of
your face in my mirror,

so long as the lights aren't out and i'm
not sinning, show up and change my life.

let me join my tolerant, patient and
loving husband in his religion,

and possibly become stronger as a unit in our marriage.

show up and make me believe.

if believing really was seeing, i'd have seen you everywhere around me as a kid,

and for a while, i did, as you were once an actual,

(and looking back this is funny to say,) imaginary friend of mine.

please be real. please explain all these questions and mysteries.

save humanity just by showing up,

like some bruce willis-esque hero that saves the day as soon as he gets there.

i guess i've always believed in god because i've always been afraid not to,

and because it works better with my worldview and my poetry if he exists.

i get hope from saying god has a plan for me,

and i can remember times he brought me through.

but then there are times i wonder, did he?

or was it just me, or us?

i could go on and on, but it's getting late.

if i see you, everything changes, but as it stands, i am still solidly an agnostic.

every once in a while, i'll wonder if i'm an atheist yet, but nah.

god forbid i stop believing completely.

i really need something to cling to right now, and i always will,

even if it turns out that i am being a bit delusional.

maybe that's it.

maybe they need you to be real.

maybe inviting jesus into your heart is accepting the notion

that your soul needs an anchor around which to gravitate,

so you don't spin away into alcoholism or suicide or madness or whatever.

maybe jesus was real, and we've just embellished upon his existence

because his life was good enough to do so,

the story old enough to ambiguously fuck with and still retain credibility, and the setting perfect enough for american holidays to exploit it.

whatever the case may be, i don't expect to really literally see his face in anything.

any sign would be great.

but enough vague interpretations of life events as signs,

i want something big and impossible to miss.

i'll be waiting with eyes open and hopeful, and a heart cynical and jaded, but curious.

don't let me down.

i want another miracle besides myself, and i'm bold enough to sit here at cvs,

a worthless, and infinitesimally finite and small peon in the eyes of the cosmos,

and still demand that the lord our god, king of fucking kings do so.

why?

because, as i believe it to be right now, that's just how he made me.

only god knows why.

proof. part two. (letter to a gracious messiah.)

ask, and it shall be given to you, seek and ye shall find...

well played, sir. well played.

almost two weeks ago, i wrote jesus/god a public letter,

yet another of my agnostic outcries for proof and less ambiguity.

well, last wednesday night was my first night by myself as an "office angel,"

volunteering at my church office, answering phones and the like.

a homeless man came in and asked me if this was a church, and if we had any food,

and said he had walked there from denton. that's a really long walk.

i could smell him as soon as he walked in the door, and my heart went out to him,

especially when the usher that came to help sent him away,

as our food pantry, or "iCare," was not open until morning.

he needed to get to a place called "the
bridge,"

a local homeless shelter with food and
resources for the homeless.

of course, no one from the church could
take him. they sent him away.

now, this is not a reflection of the
church, they help many people,

they were just unable to help at that
time. i felt horrible,

as i watched him walk away, despondent,
tired, and hungry.

i've always had a big heart about this
kind of thing, and wished i could help
more.

i discussed it with randy, who had set
up right behind me at the desk,

browsing online on the church's wifi,
and our computer.

he agreed to run the man to where he had
to go, if it wasn't too far.

we didn't have much gas at the time. for
thirty minutes he looked outside for
that man,

unable to find him anywhere. every time
he stood at the door and shook his head,

i felt worse and worse. i began to cry. full-on bawling in the church office. you see,

i remember when a couple of months ago, we had no food or money,

and went to this same church office for help, and were turned away. again,

nothing they could've done, but the seeds of wanting to change that began to come into being.

now, they were in full bloom, and i was feeling a calling by god to do something about it.

anyway, back to the story, after a while, randy came in and sat down,

and we both felt like shit. some minutes later, to my ecstatic joy, he came back in,

and i immediately told him that my husband randy would take him to the bridge,

which it turns out, was downtown. randy looked at me, and i told him to be careful.

i was so happy. randy took him to the bridge and he was grateful. now, i know many people would not have done this, in the interest of safety,

but let me explain something to you: #1. i am a great people reader.

i learned how do do it growing up with my mom,

and getting a bad feeling from literally every guy she ever dated or married.

this was after dad, as they divorced when i was very young, and he died in 1997.

#2. don't let fear stop you from doing what's right.

unless you get a bad feeling from the person, (i know, you can't always tell, so use discretion,)

at least try to help them in some way. i was so happy, so fulfilled,

so spiritually charged with new purpose and fervor for god and his work,

that something began to happen inside of me, and contrary to what i always believed,

it didn't take long. during the wednesday night worship service that followed, it was cemented in me that my service is my assurance, that the proof really is in the pudding,

but only if it is you who "makes it," so to speak.

it didn't matter how many theological, philosophical or personal questions i still had.

i instantly knew they would be answered in time, in his time. this had been a gradual process,

although it still seems to me so instantaneous and unexpected,

that had been at work inside me ever since i met randy and saw what a true christian was,

by his actions, not his words. he never preaches or judges, he just loves and loves in a big way.

he is my everything.

even when i challenged what i then considered to be his delusional and flawed belief system,

he never got mad, never put it in my face. he was confident in his faith,

and after a few of those discussions,

i realized that his faith was immovable
and his assurance was final and
complete.

i stopped making fun of his religion,
which i never should have done,

and i began to try to understand him.

he would even read my pieces about
doubting jesus and being bitter towards
god,

and not react in any way but love and
understanding.

clearly this man had been sent to me by
the very god i hurled by anger and
doubts at!

clearly god loves me so much that he
gave me this man,

who has loved me like i was never loved
before,

and changed my life more than anyone in
this world!

clearly god understood, and was turning
those angry and doubtful wailings into
blessings,

that are undeniably from him, so that i
may know the truth of his amazing love!

clearly, and with the same confident
assurance,

has he waited until my heart was ready to change a cynic into a believer,

no matter my cruelty or confusion! randy was the first step, and then came discovery umc,

a fantastic gay-friendly church in hoover, alabama that we are still members of.

the cold ice of my heart gave way a little at a time and i knew i was being prepared and changed,

even though at that point, and even this one, at times, that was all i was certain of.

our favorite part of discovery was the hospitality group,

which focused on the lgbt community within the church, and ways to reconcile the two.

joe openshaw is an amazing host, and we learned so much! that group is smaller without us now,

but still making a big impact. we love and miss them all.

that's where i really started to grow more, and want to know more. when we moved to dallas, it wasn't long before we discovered the beacon of awesomeness and love and yes, hope,

that is cathedral of hope. it catered to my artistic side, randy could finally join a choir again,

and we were the majority. i immediately loved it and set about getting involved.

at the present time, we are members, randy's in choir, and i am a greeter, an office angel,

run my own monthly open mic there, and am trying to get involved now in the iCare ministry.

my spiritual growth exploded, but of course, i was still a strict agnostic,

and i saw nothing that could possibly change that.

this brings me back to wanting to change things at cathedral, so that homeless people,

and economically disadvantaged people could get food and help

when "icare," is closed or unable to help.

i want to fill in the cracks where they leave off, so that NO ONE is turned away.

i don't know yet how it would work, or even if they'll allow me to do it,

but i am meeting with the associate pastor soon and i'm going to try.

i'm thinking of calling it "soul food,"

because the greatest witness to people is compassion and selflessness,

and because of the obvious food and church connotations.

anyway, back to my transformation, i will soon ask to be baptized,

because i know that this church is where god wants me,

and this heart is what god wants me to use. as far as my doubts and questions,

of course, they didn't go away. but god, i'm assured, will answer them in time.

even if i fail, and i know i will backslide at times, and even if this isn't the way,

i am reminded of, despite the church's stance,

the profoundly insightful and understanding words of a sunday school teacher

at a church that wound up denying us because we were a couple,

"even if this isn't the way, (christianity,) it's a light in the darkness,

and if it doesn't work for you, i encourage you to find another light.

try it out, and if it doesn't work for you, go find what does."

i'm paraphrasing but you get the general idea.

yesterday i got c.s. lewis's books, "mere christianity, and "surprised by joy,"

for more insight on my transformation, by reading about his.

i am enjoying the latter book thus far.

i also got a point/counterpoint book called, "god?"

that had a debate between a christian and an atheist,

and a book called "varieties of unbelief," that also looked up my alley, so to speak.

all i know is, i feel better, i know i am called to serve others, via my poetry and my service,

and i am a better man than i was yesterday.

not because i "got religion and saw the light, praise jesus,"

but because i want to be, and for the first time in ages, i'm really listening.

i asked for jesus christ to show his face, but through me,

his face was seen by a man in desperate need. that's good enough for me.

christ or no christ, mythology or no mythology, bible or no bible,

i don't want to just do good works,

i see good works being done in me, and it's not always me.

now, am i gonna go and erase every agnostic or doubtful piece or post i've ever written?

hell no. they made excellent points. i'm still me. i'm just a lot happier.

if it works for you, i say go with it. and you know,

---

it's not despite my previous doubt and
agnosticism,

and anger that i am a better person now,

but because of what i went through,

and who i was that makes me an even
better candidate

for the love and life-changing mercy of
jesus christ.

it makes for a more compelling testimony
as well.

paul used to kill christians, but look
at who he became,

through a transformation of god.

because of who i was and what i've been
through, i bring with me,

into this new frontier, an open mind, a
courageous heart, a questioning
curiosity,

a new-found respect for my patient and
graceful savior,

and the intelligence, wit, humor and
spirit that have always

been hallmarks of my astounding
existence.

there is no judgment here, because i once stood on the stony gravel of rock bottom,

and demanded more of god, shouting my obscenities and disappointments into the night.

and i stand here now, nowhere near complete, but once again at the beginning of this journey,

ready to embark upon the destination he has set for me. and i'm happy.

it's funny, two weeks ago, i was closer to atheism than anything else. and you know what?

i'm not gonna sit here in this cafe typing this, and bag on atheism,

as if i'd have made some grim mistake if i'd have gone down that road.

some of my favorite people, comics, and writers are atheists and i love them to death.

i would've been proud to be an atheist, if i had decided that was what i was. it just wasn't.

the existence of god, even when i doubted all else and hated him,

was just never a question for me.

i just knew. i've always known. i don't feel the need to prove it,

even though i actually agree with a lot of atheist's points sometimes.

and another thing, legitimate unbiased science is something we should couple every religion with,

but not something to be fused with a religion,

because then you have bias, which never leads to truth.

look, all i know and believe, and even before my transformation, have believed,

is that i want to help people, and right some wrongs that i believe are being ignored.

do i believe in heaven and hell? well first, i believe,

as i've said before in less assured pieces about god,

that we make our own here on earth. but whether or not they exist,

or are just spiritual and theological incentives to do good, is not the point of doing good AT ALL.

i don't help you because later, i'll get something i want,

or because i'm afraid that if i don't
help you,

i'll burn forever in a lake of fire that
god supposedly made for bad people.

i help you because i'm not in it for me!
wow! what a concept! christian
selflessness!

i didn't learn that was real from any
church, but from my husband.

i help you because i've been there, but
even if i haven't, you need help,

and how about this, IT'S THE RIGHT THING
TO DO!

regardless of what any religion
describes as wrong or right,

human decency and compassion are always
the right way to live your life.

not feigned humanity or compassion for
show, but doing selfless shit,

(ooooh, you cussed! again, same bear,)
when nobody is watching. anyway, really
long story short,

i desperately asked for proof of
christ's existence, and a mere three
days later, i got it,

in the way it mattered most. he exists
in me, through my service.

i am assured of the heaven i make for myself and others.

i am saved because, in my compassion, i reached out to touch god through touching others,

and finally broke my chains. freedom means giving the key away.

maybe this is the key, maybe not, but he's the only light i see,

this amazing christ that once was a symbol of judgment and hate,

because of the bigotry of others, is really a god of grace and compassion, poetry and light,

patience and understanding, majesty and humility, good works and glitter.

and i love being all of those things for someone else.

and besides, everyone could do with more glitter!

thank you god. thanks for letting me question everything,

because it has just made the answer more glorious and wonderful.

thanks for the proof, which i now realize, was always, ALWAYS me.

the proof is me, lord.

and the answer is you.

i get it.

i finally get it.

i love you too.

parts.

she had two hearts when she loved me.

she had twelve fingers when she
scratched my back.

she had eight eyes when she cried, and
four when she laughed.

she had eleven tongues when the clock
struck twelve.

she had three hands, or maybe six, when
she loved me.

she had twenty backbones when she
defended me,

and none when she looked in the mirror.

she had one voice that sounded like two
when she cried out.

she had a thousand feet when she ran.

she had five pairs of breasts when she
loved me.

there was more of her than i could ever
count or appreciate,

when she loved me.

but she doesn't anymore, and all i have
left of her is one whole heart;

leftover pieces from the two that i
broke.

Thursday.

(for all the gods anywhere that are one
with death inside.)

Thursday is for waiting,

thursday is a hammer,

thursday is a painting,

that only shows with blood.

thursday is for thunder,

thursday is for floods,

thursday is a sunset,

one smeared with glory and pain.

thursday is a breaking,

thursday is for the insane,

thursday is for escaping,

anywhere not as free as whispers.

thursday is for mistresses,

thursday is a mister,

thursday is a longing,

with desperate fingers reaching for
friday.

thursday is not your day,

thursday is not my day,

thursday asks twenty-four hours,

"are the lost gods returning?"

thursday is a freezing,

thursday is a burning,

thursday is a grim hurricane,

for only the dead are blown away.

thursday is a feeling,

thursday is not a day,

thursday is revealing,

all the secrets you've yet to make.

thursday is for gloating,

thursday is for mistakes,

thursday is an abyss, floating:

death, suspended in the stars.

thursday is for the wounded,

thursday is for scars,

thursday is a tomb,

inside of mother mary, quaking.

thursday is for wanting,

thursday is for aching,

thursday is for Thor's day,

gods were flesh that became the word.

thursday is a prophet,

thursday is a blackbird,

Thursday was the first day;

the big bang started with a stammer.

i miss you, i miss you.

i have a heart of stone,
and it needs to break,
free from this heavy feeling,
i miss you, i miss you,
touch me, open the scar,
pull out my heart,
turn stone back to blood,
i miss you, i miss you.
your heart is a kite,
and i'm holding your string down,
with mine, how it wants to rise,
i miss you, i miss you,
phone calls turn me inside out,
my tears run from this pain,
your voice a thousand miles away,
i miss you, i miss you,
it's snowing where you are,
how is it i am colder?
your footsteps melt the snow,
i miss you, i miss you.
this poem is so very trite,

my hands fumble at the keyboard,

pulsing out heartbeats of stone,

i miss you, i miss you,

there's so much in the way,

even when you're here with me,

if only i were someone else,

i miss you, i miss you,

social constraints, and obligations,

the circles that never fully meet,

i'd rearrange my world if only,

i miss you, i miss you,

the fates see us another way,

a way it maybe is meant to be,

still, you should know you healed my
heart,

i miss you, i miss you,

trembling here with my book of poems,

i feel the stone fall away and crumble,

i love you, there is no other way,

i miss you, i miss you.

Acknowledgements.

Randy, You are my north star. All my life I prayed for someone like you, and all of a sudden there you were. Your amazing love and unconditional support have made my life the best it's ever been, and are the cornerstones of this amazing work of art. Thanks for always being there for me, and being my constant supporter. I love you, babe. They say love is the greatest adventure of all, and that has certainly proved to be true with us. I can't wait to wake up next to you for the rest of my life, and join you on this strangely wonderful adventure we call life.

Mom, I wanna thank you for all your support and for your steadfast belief in me during our dark times. Thanks also for encouraging that little boy who loved books and poetry. Look at him now, Mom, he's all grown up and finally has his book. I love you. I can't wait to see you and Morgan and Laikyn again.

Eric, you are and always have been my brother. I remember all the fun times we had in high school: hanging out together, reading George Carlin books, listening to Beatles' lyrics until the sun came up, and writing poetry about America and the system we were just discovering was broken. You were always there for me, and when you found Amber I was ecstatic for you. If any two people were soul-mates, it would be you two. I have watched like a proud big brother as you two have achieved so much together, and I know that I can always count on you. Thanks brother, for loving me despite my monsters and for supporting this book as much as you have.

Amber, I am so proud to call you my sister. My brother Eric has been through a lot of heartache in his life, and it does my soul good to know he has someone like you. You are his bright and morning star, and I thank God every single day for you. But that's not the only reason, because I also thank God for your friendship. You have been nothing but kind to Randy and I and in the midst of your struggling as a young married couple, you and Eric took us into your home when you didn't have to, and frankly, didn't need to. Thanks for doing the hard thing, the right thing. We love yall for it. Thanks for being my cheerleader, and for your support of this book. You guys mean the world to me.

Corey, you were my first boyfriend
during a time when I was just
discovering the other side of myself,
and accepting it. You've been one of my
best friends for a long time, and you've
always supported and advised me. You're
so mature for your age, and so wise and
I'm thankful for everything you've done
for me. If I were the president, you
would most certainly be my advisor.
You're also one of the sweetest guys on
the planet, as well as one of the most
modest. I love that about you. I also
love the fact that you're such a big
geek. If you were a comic book
character, you would be superman in a
batman costume. Thanks for all your
love, advice, and support.

Dez, you are my best friend, my mentor, and my partner-in-crime. You introduced me to Dallas, and all the open mics, including Mad Swirl, and to some amazing poets. You taught me to write my truth, and ever since then, it has become my mantra. You have done so much for me, inside and out, that I don't have enough room here to say it all. Thanks for everything, and thanks for inspiring some of my best works. You're family, and I know you'll always be there for me, no matter what. I love you. This book would suck without you, sissy.

Mk, ever since we met at a poetry slam in Montevallo, AL, you have amazed and astounded me with the depths and heights and breadths of your poetry. Between that and your wonderful sweet personality, it didn't take us long to become best friends We are now as close as family, and I wouldn't have it any other way. Reading your amazing poetry has helped inspire a few of these works, as well as reading many of the brilliant poets you've introduced me to. I will always love you for your sweetness, for your friendship, and for your genius. Thanks for everything, Mk.

Lilly, you are the person that besides myself, has worked hardest on this book. Thank you for all your help editing, formatting, and advising on this book. Without you this book would not look as good as it does. Thank you for your constant dedication and friendship, and thank you for keeping me on task. I miss you and I hope to hang out with you soon. I am proud to have Penhall Publishing as this book's publisher. It is an honor.

Christian. For anyone reading this book who enjoys its cover, an amazing and artistic portrait of me, they need only thank the phenomenal artist, Christian Millet. I contracted him to do this beautiful piece a few years back, anticipating the need for a great book cover for my first book of poetry. I had seen many of his works online, and they frankly took my breath away. As a big lover of modern art, and having fallen in love with his style of painting, I knew he was the perfect man for the job. He certainly did not disappoint, and so Christian, I would like to thank you for your work on this beautiful piece of art, and for working with me to ensure that my needs were met. I highly encourage all of my readers to follow him on facebook and to support his art.

Rosie. I wanna thank a special friend of mine who is a wonderful photographer, Rosie Lindsey. Thank you, Rosie for taking my photo shoot in that bookstore. They look great! One of those great high quality photos was chosen to be my back cover. Thanks for your photography and support. I really appreciate it. I would highly recommend anyone in the DFW area to contract you for all of their photography needs!

Mad Swirl, you guys have been my open mic home for a long time. When I lived in Alabama, I would visit Dallas with Dez, who is the one who introduced me to the swirly awesomeness that is the Mad Swirl open mic! I fell in love with it, and the people involved. **Johnny Q** and **Mh Clay** have created a world where the artist is free to be themselves, and showcase their art or poetry. Every time I visited Dallas with Dez, and during my six month stay in Dallas in 2009, I couldn't wait to get my monthly dose of Swirl. When I moved here for good last year, Mad Swirl was a big part of the reason why. Going to Mad Swirl and being exposed to so much great poetry and so many amazing poets helped shape me into the poet I am. Many of the pieces in this book would not exist without you guys. I have submitted to madswirl.com many times and I thank them for their time and attention not only with me and my works, but everyone's. It really is a great site where artists and poets from around the world submit, get read, and get fans they would not have without madswirl.com. If you're in the area, and love poetry, art, or want to create a fan-base for your work, Mad Swirl is the place to start!

God. Last, but certainly not least, is
God. Without God, I wouldn't be here,
and neither would this book. I have been
through so much in my life, and at my
lowest of lows, He was there driving me
onward to keep going, and never give up.
He gave me this indescribably useful and
wonderful gift, and whether I used it to
praise Him, question Him, or outright
damn Him, He waited patiently while I
matured as a poet, and realized His
love. I haven't always had the best
relationship with God, but He's always
been there, orchestrating events in my
life to make it better, even though I
couldn't see it. He never gave me the
easy choice, I always had to prove
myself ready for the next level. I am so
thankful for that, because it made me
stronger. Some of the hardest times in
my life helped mold me into the man I am
today, a man of integrity, and I am
still being molded. I wanna thank you,
God for loving me when I didn't love
myself, and helping me through the dark
times so I could find the light inside
myself. Thank you most of all for this

book, my dream come true. It wasn't
easy, and at one point, I had to start
all over. I remember thinking it would
never happen. But now I'm here, standing
on the precipice of this glorious dream,
and knowing full well how many people
this book will help. I pray you use it,
even though it's as dirty and funny and
completely inappropriate as I am,
because I know it's also as sweet, and
hopeful, and passionate, and persistent
as I am. I pray you use it to help
people, get them to see the light in the
darkness, make them bust out laughing,
drive them to tears if need be, and to
let other poets know that they can do it
too if they just keep working at it.
Thank you God also for these amazing
people you've put in my life, as well as
my friends and family. You know what
you're doing in and through me, and I
just hope I am wise enough now to shut
up, trust you, and let you do your
thing. I love you.

About James Barrett Rodehaver

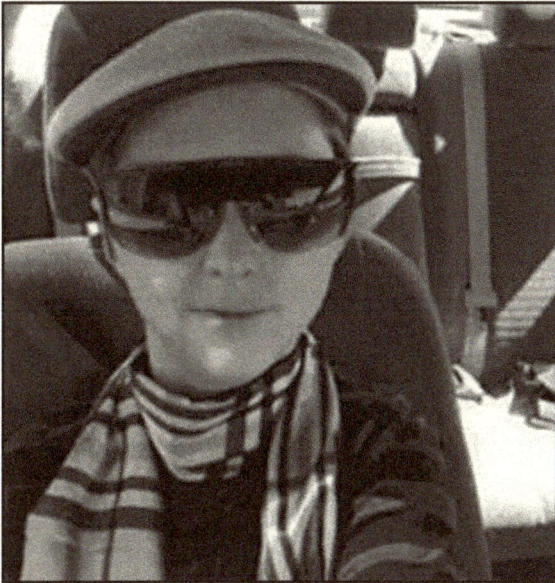

James Barrett Rodehaver, also known by his popular nickname, "Bear," is a 30 year old poet living in Dallas, Texas. An Alabama native, and lifelong poet, Bear is a prolific, engaging, eye-opening writer whose verses show levels of bravery, humor and depth that are far beyond his years.

Born on life support, and going through three months in a coma as a baby, he rose like a phoenix in spite of doctor's claims. Enduring an incredible life of adversity, he has gone through many trials, such as growing up in a broken family, two foster homes, seven surgeries, (including open heart,) a divorce, coming out as bisexual, and dealing with his disability every day.

He is supposed to be dead many times over. Bear has a very rare bone disease which gets progressively worse as he ages, and causes a number of debilitating symptoms, including complete hypothyroidism. Because of this, he looks and sounds years younger than he is, and must take external hormones; the paradox being that the bone disease makes him feel like an old man. He also suffers from mild right hand nerve damage. Because of his condition he has used canes, wheelchairs, and walkers at different times in his life. Nowadays, he walks with a cane most of the time.

His passion and perseverance is a testament to his willpower, and courage. He has written poetry since he was seven years old, and it is his life. Now a full-grown man, and a fully developed poet, he spends his time reading, writing poetry a lot, collecting books, watching his favorite shows on TV, as well as going to the movies and the theatre. He also enjoys hanging with his friends, singing karaoke, going to open mics in dallas, and (very) amateur photography. He loves many foods, but none more than seafood, as his mother's side of the family hails from Louisiana. He will try any food at least once.

He loves great music, and has very eclectic music tastes, but none more than good ol' rock n' roll. Bear is a rocker at heart, loving classic rock, alternative rock, and any other good modern rock. He has led an amazing and poetic life, and continues to share his legacy of love with his words.